HARRY TIEBOUT
The Collected Writings

HARRY TIEBOUT

The Collected Writings

 Hazelden
Publishing

Hazelden Publishing
Center City, Minnesota 55012-0176
hazelden.org/bookstore

Library of Congress Cataloging-in-Publication Data

Tiebout, Harry, 1896–1966.
    [Selections. 1999]
    Harry Tiebout : the collected writings.
      p. cm.
    Includes bibliographical references.
    ISBN 1-56838-345-2
    1. Alcoholism. I. Title.
  RC565.T54   1999
  616.86'1—dc21   99-36844
                                          CIP

Editor's note
Minor editing has been done to these essays in accordance with Hazelden
editorial style and grammatical usage.

Interior design by Donna Burch
Typesetting by Stanton Publication Services, Inc.

Contents

Introduction

Harry Morgan Tiebout was the first psychiatrist to publicly recognize and uphold the work of Alcoholics Anonymous. He was born January 2, 1896, in Brooklyn, New York. After graduating from Wesleyan College in 1917, he attended medical school at Johns Hopkins University. There he interned and specialized in psychiatry. In 1922, he joined the staff at Westchester Division of the New York Hospital, where he remained until 1924. Thereafter, until 1935, he practiced psychiatry at various centers for child guidance. That year, he became director of Blythewood Sanitarium, Greenwich, Connecticut; and it was there that alcoholism became the primary concern of his professional career.

Tiebout is uniquely distinguished for having facilitated communication between the worlds of alcoholism and psychiatry. He made psychiatric knowledge of alcoholism available to the lay public in language they could understand. Conversely, he was almost solely responsible for bringing the principles and philosophy of Alcoholics Anonymous—which represented a major advance in alcoholic rehabilitation—to the attention of the psychiatric world.

In 1939, Tiebout was introduced to AA. Until that year, success had generally resisted his best efforts in the clinical treatment of the alcoholic. Then, suddenly, two of his patients experienced dramatic recoveries using the suggested program of AA. Tiebout investigated it. One of these patients was Marty Mann, whose story appears in the Big Book as "Women Suffer Too." The results of his long-term AA study, published in the *American Journal of Psychiatry,* were the now-famous papers on ego reduction and surrender in the alcoholic recovery process.

Tiebout consistently worked to have his views concerning alcoholism accepted by the medical and psychiatric professions. He acknowledged publicly that since 1939, when he had become an observer of AA, his own approach to alcoholism had undergone an almost total reorientation. During the years when AA was experiencing its first growth, he endorsed its program to his psychiatric colleagues. In 1944, he was instrumental in persuading the American Medical Society of New York to hear a paper by one of the cofounders of AA, Bill Wilson. Five years later, he again arranged to have Wilson address the medical profession—this time the American Psychiatric Association.

For more than a quarter century Tiebout played an active part in the affairs of AA. As an internationally renowned expert on alcoholism, he continued to promote the acceptance of AA in the medical profession. He served on the Board of Trustees for Alcoholics Anonymous from 1957 to 1966; he was chairman of the National Council on Alcoholism in 1950 and president of the same organization from 1951 to 1953.

Harry Morgan Tiebout, at age seventy, died April 2, 1966.

> Dr. Harry M. Tiebout, 70, one of the first psychiatrists to advance the theory that alcoholism is a disease rather than an immorality or crime, died Saturday in Greenwich Hospital after a heart attack. He lived at 215 Milbank Ave. and had an office at 49 Lake Ave.
>
> Dr. Tiebout set forth his views on alcoholism

in 1946, when he was a member of the staff of Blythewood Sanatorium here, in an article in "The Quarterly Journal of Studies of Alcohol."

Dr. Tiebout also was one of the first psychiatrists to endorse, without qualification, Alcoholics Anonymous as an agent in controlling compulsive drinking, because of the group's belief that a victim must first "surrender to a higher power" before achieving day-by-day abstinence. He addressed the 1955 convention of Alcoholics Anonymous in St. Louis in 1955, and had been a trustee of the organization since 1957.

He also was president of the National Committee on Alcoholism, and helped form the Connecticut Commission on Alcoholism, serving as its vice chairman from 1952 to 1957. He was former chairman of the American Psychiatric Association's committee on alcoholism and was a member of the advisory panel on mental health and alcoholism for the World Health Organization in Geneva from 1954 to 1959.

In addition he was a fellow of the American Orthopsychiatric Association, former president of the Connecticut Society of Psychiatry and Neurology, the New York Psychiatric Society, and the Society of Psychopathology and Psychotherapy.

Born in Brooklyn, he was graduated from Wesleyan University in 1917 and obtained his medical degree from Johns Hopkins University in 1921. Before coming here, he was a member of the staff of the Westchester Division of New York Hospital, in White Plains.

Surviving are his wife, Mrs. Ethel M. Mills Tiebout; two sons, Charles M. and Harry M. Tiebout Jr.; a daughter, Mrs. P. Ross Warn; a sister, Mrs. Spencer Reeder; and 10 grandchildren.[1]

In Memory of Harry[1]

By the time this issue of the *Grapevine* reaches its readers, the whole world of AA will have heard of the passing of our well-beloved friend, Dr. Harry M. Tiebout, the first psychiatrist ever to hold up the hands of our Fellowship for all to see. His gifts of courageous example, deep perception of our needs, and constant labor in our behalf have been—and always will be—values quite beyond our reckoning.

It began like this: The year was early 1939, and the book *Alcoholics Anonymous* was about to hit the press. To help with the final edit of that volume we had made prepublication copies in multigraph form. One of them fell into Harry's hands. Though much of the content was then alien to his own views, he read our upcoming book with deep interest. Far more significantly, he at once resolved to show the new volume to a couple of his patients, since known to us as "Marty" and "Grenny." These were the toughest kind of customers, and seemingly hopeless.

At first, the book made little impression on this pair. Indeed, its heavy larding with the word *God* so angered Marty that she threw it out her window, flounced off the grounds of the swank sanatorium where she was, and proceeded to tie on a big bender.

Grenny didn't carry a rebellion quite so far; he played it cool.

When Marty finally turned up, shaking badly, and asked Dr. Harry what next to do, he simply grinned and

1

said, "You'd better read that book again!" Back in her quarters, Marty finally brought herself to leaf through its pages once more. A single phrase caught her eye and it read, "We cannot live with resentment." The moment she admitted this to herself, she was filled with a "transforming spiritual experience."

Forthwith she attended a meeting. It was at Clinton Street, Brooklyn, where Lois and I lived. Returning to Blythewood she found Grenny intensely curious. Her first words to him were these: "Grenny, we are not alone anymore!"

This was the beginning of recovery for both—recoveries that have lasted until this day. Watching their unfoldment, Harry was electrified. Only a week before they had both presented stone walls of obstinate resistance to his every approach. Now they talked, and freely. To Harry these were the facts—and brand-new facts. Scientist and man of courage that he was, Harry did not for a moment look the other way. Setting aside his own convictions about alcoholism and its neurotic manifestations, he soon became convinced that AA had something, perhaps something big.

All the years afterwards, and often at very considerable risk to his professional standing, Harry continued to endorse AA. Considering Harry's professional standing, this required courage of the highest order.

Let me share some concrete examples. In one of his early medical papers—that noted one on Surrender[2]—he had declared this ego-reducing practice to be not only basic to AA, but also absolutely fundamental to his own practice of psychiatry. This took humility as well as fortitude. It will always be a bright example for us all.

Nevertheless this much was but a bare beginning. In 1944, helped by Dr. Kirby Collier of Rochester and

Dwight Anderson of New York, Harry persuaded the American Medical Society of the State of New York to let me, a layman, read a paper about AA, at their annual gathering. Five years later this same trio, again spearheaded by Harry, persuaded the American Psychiatric Association to invite the reading of another paper by me—this time in their 1949 Annual Meeting at Montreal. By then, AA had about 100,000 members, and many psychiatrists had already seen at close range our impact on their patients.

For us of AA who were present at that gathering it was a breathtaking hour. My presentation would be the "spiritual experience," as we AAs understood it. Surely we could never get away with this! To our astonishment the paper was extremely well received—judging, at least, from the sustained applause.

Immediately afterwards, I was approached by a most distinguished old gentleman. He introduced himself as an early president of the American Psychiatric Association. Beaming he said, "Mr. W., it is very possible that I am the only one of my colleagues here today who really believes in 'spiritual experience' as you do. Once upon a time, I myself had an awakening much akin to your own, an experience that I shared in common with two close friends, Bucke and Whitman."

Naturally I inquired, "But why did your colleagues seem to like the paper?"

His reply went like this: "You see, we psychiatrists deeply know what very difficult people you alcoholics really are. It was not the claims of your paper that stirred my friends, it was the fact that AA can sober up alcoholics wholesale."

Seen in this light, I was the more deeply moved by the generous and magnificent tribute that had been paid to us of AA. My paper was soon published in the *American Psychiatric Journal* and our New York headquarters was authorized by the Association to make all the reprints we wished for distribution. By then the trek of AA overseas had well begun. Heaven only knows what this invaluable reprint accomplished when it was presented to psychiatrists in distant places by the fledgling AA groups. It vastly hastened the worldwide acceptance of AA.

I could go on and on about Harry, telling you of his activities and in the general field of alcoholism, of his signal service on our AA Board of Trustees. I could tell stories of my own delightful friendship with him, especially remembering his great good humor and infectious laugh. But the space allotted me is too limited.

So in conclusion, I would have Harry speak for himself. Our *AA Grapevine* of November 1963 carried a piece by him that, between its lines, unconsciously reveals to us a wonderful self-portrait of our friend. Again, we feel his fine perception, again we see him at work for AA. No epitaph could be better than this.

—BILL W.

The Role of Psychiatry in the Field of Alcoholism, with Comment on the Concept of Alcoholism as Symptom and as Disease[1]

Interest in alcoholism is growing rapidly in many directions. State legislatures have adopted new laws, or are considering bills, with provisions ranging from investigative commissions to well-established programs of treatment and research. National organizations have sprung up that stress the need for public education and for study of the many issues presented. The police and other correctional agencies are less and less disposed to treat the alcoholic offender as a criminal; they welcome the signs of a more rational approach to the problem. The continued growth of Alcoholics Anonymous has helped to arouse general awareness of the problem and to spread the knowledge that alcoholism is no longer the hopeless scourge that motivated the Prohibition experiment.

The problem itself looms large statistically on the psychiatric horizon. The data usually cited refer to several million excessive drinkers, among whom at least 750,000 exhibit manifest signs of alcoholic diseases. The numbers of alcoholics become more impressive when compared with the 500,000 known to have tuberculosis. No one can question the overall importance of the problem of alcoholism.

Where does psychiatry fit into the picture? One answer may be derived from a field outside the field of psychiatry. In a pamphlet entitled "Principles for Public

Action on Problem Drinking," with the subheading "A Guide to Model Legislation," issued in 1947 by the Research Council on Problems of Alcohol, that organization listed seven principles of action without once using the word *psychiatry* or *psychiatrist*. The only reference to the psychiatric side of the problem reads: "Existing mental hospitals should accept as patients, either directly or by referral from general hospitals, those problem drinkers whose abnormal drinking is purely symptomatic, i.e., the psychotic, the feebleminded, and others." The custodial contribution is all that was recognized. Although the Research Council no longer exists, the depreciation of the role that psychiatry may play in the resolution of the problem of alcoholism presumably survives. It is important because this evaluation arises not from animosity toward psychiatry but from a belief that psychiatry has too little to offer to merit consideration. That belief rests, obviously, on the insufficient contribution of psychiatry in this field in the past. The analysis of the reasons for this insufficiency constitutes the main objective of the present communication.

Two factors may account for the present state of affairs. First, the peculiar difficulties of the problem of alcoholism have discouraged psychiatrists from studying it with sufficient intensity; second, the psychiatrists have labored under certain faulty theoretical assumptions that have handicapped them in coming to grips with the practical issues.

As to the first point, the alcoholic is a difficult patient for psychiatrists to learn about. If the alcoholic is in an institution, he clamors to get out and usually succeeds, since he is not psychotic. If he is at liberty he seldom maintains a routine treatment relationship; he thus affords few of the usual opportunities for deeper insight. Moreover, as a rule he seeks help only when prostrated by liquor, and then it is likely to be at such inconvenient hours that he is avoided as not only a most unpromising candidate for therapy but also an out-and-out nuisance. In consequence, few psychiatrists have had an opportunity to develop a solid body of knowledge concerning the condition.

The second and perhaps more serious block to formulating an adequate working concept of the condition may be found in certain erroneous assumptions concerning its nature. Although it is frequently stated that alcoholism is a disease, psychiatrists as a rule have not really accorded it that status but have most often held it to be a symptom of some underlying condition that must be uncovered before rational treatment can be instituted.

Since the underlying condition is almost always assumed to be one of the already known mental deviations, the psychiatrist, operating on that belief, tends to sidestep the drinking to search for the underlying disease and the causative factors involved in its production. The drinking is merely a sign of depression, of elation, of withdrawal, or of some neurotic complication. Anyone who stops to study a symptom is thought to be therapeutically naive and in need of some instruction about first principles.

While therapy directed toward the cause of a condition is ideal, total neglect of the symptom may result in ineffective therapy. The symptom itself may assume disease proportions. This may be illustrated by analogy with fever.[2]

Nowadays no one treats a fever. One looks for the causative agent and treats for that, knowing that the fever will subside if its cause can be eradicated. Occasionally, however, the fever gets out of hand and becomes in and

of itself a threat to the patient's life. At that point, regardless of cause, the fever itself must be reduced below
the level where it threatens life. In the beginning the
fever could be considered a symptom and could be safely
ignored as an object of therapy. It may, however, over-
whelm the clinical picture, and when it does it must become the aim of treatment if the patient is to survive. To
continue to focus on the cause in the face of the immediate threat to life would be therapeutic folly.

Another analogy may be cited. Irritation may produce
some form of cancer; or, to put it differently, cancer may
be a reaction to or a symptom of irritation of some sort.
Once the cancer process has started, however, removal of
the irritation does not stay it. The abnormal growth proceeds unchecked and it must be attacked directly. In other
words, what started as a symptomatic response finally assumes disease significance and we then treat it as an in-
dependent illness.

The same thinking is valid for alcoholism. It, too, is a
symptom that has taken on disease significance. Though
starting as a symptom of underlying factors, it gains mo-
mentum until it gets out of hand and becomes a disease
in itself. To insist on treatment of the original causes is
like focusing upon the cause of the life-threatening fever
or upon the irritation leading to cancer. The cause and
the origins are irrelevant to the immediate danger.

One clinical fact supports the conclusion that alcoholism is a symptom that has become a disease. Experience repeatedly proves that no amount of probing and
unraveling allows a return to normal drinking. Once the
state of alcoholism has supervened, it seems to remove any
later possibility of controlled drinking. This new element
survives as if it were a sensitized phenomenon, sure to be
touched off sooner or later if drinking is attempted. The

alcoholic always harbors the disease potential once that potential has come into being. He is forever susceptible.

Further evidence for regarding alcoholism as an illness in and of itself may be seen in the experience of Alcoholics Anonymous. Part of the success of that organization undoubtedly rests upon its simple assumption that alcoholism is the condition to be combated. Undeterred by technical scientific considerations and making no pretense of ferreting out causes, they tackle the alcoholism and succeed more often than they fail. Initially the stress is entirely upon getting the individual to admit that he is an alcoholic. The First Step of their program reads: "We admitted we were powerless over alcohol—that our lives had become unmanageable." A speaker at their meetings introduces himself and then states, "I am an alcoholic." While it is true that they have learned that the way to maintain abstinence is through developing the capacity to live soberly, their earliest efforts are essentially limited to helping the alcoholic accept the fact that he can no longer drink normally and that he can no longer safely take even one drink. This direct approach works and works sufficiently often to justify the belief that it is founded on one of the fundamental aspects of alcoholism.

If the technique by which this result is effected is examined, it can be seen to resemble a formula that the Alcoholics Anonymous members can follow on a prescription basis, as it were. If, they say, you accept that you are an alcoholic, do this and do that and you will discover you will not be troubled by a desire to take a drink. Instead of an operation to cut out the disease, they have a program that seems to remove the pressure to drink. Concentrating solely on the immediate problem of alcohol, and treating the alcoholic's drinking itself as a disease to be eliminated, they seem to have found a remedy for the ailment, alcoholism. Their program, of course, also provides Steps for the maintenance of the sobriety once achieved, but the initial Steps and the initial emphasis are all upon getting the individual to acknowledge and accept his alcoholism.

The simile between cancer and alcoholism may be carried a little further. No one questions the wisdom of operating when a cancer is discovered, even if the irritation that caused it is known. Nor is it held to be therapeutically naive to tackle the emerging symptom directly as an entity needing correction. Regardless of cause, the cancer itself must be removed.

Paralleling this, may not alcoholism be considered a disease that emerges from past psychic irritations? The Alcoholics Anonymous program, attacking the drinking directly, is similar in effect to the operation for cancer.

The suspicion of naïveté should perhaps be directed toward those who stick to the theoretical assumption that alcoholism is merely a symptom and who hold this view in the face of facts that seem to support a different interpretation. One of the chief complaints registered by alcoholics in respect to psychiatrists is that the latter never talk about drinking and seem neither interested nor concerned about its concrete manifestations—sprees and hangovers, the dawning realization of a change in the drinking pattern, the various futile attempts to recapture the former capacity for control. The alcoholic intuitively feels that his drinking is the immediate seat of trouble, and so he waves away the findings of a psychiatrist who calls it "merely" a symptom. Not until the disease concept is grasped can the psychiatrist really empathize the alcoholic's state of mind as a victim of the condition. Until he does, the psychiatrist will always seem a little remote and talking at cross-purposes. The psychiatrist may consider the so-called compulsive element as the crystallization of the disease potential into actuality. With this viewpoint the problem of alcoholism becomes not only much easier to understand but also much more responsive to therapeutic efforts.

In advancing this concept of the nature of alcoholism, there is no thought of denying or belittling the importance of psychotherapy on the deepest possible level. Such therapy, however, must aim at helping the individual to learn to live with his limitation, namely, that he cannot drink normally. The alcoholic must be brought to accept that he is the victim of a disease and that the only way for him to remain healthy is to refrain from taking the first drink; that if he attempts to drink moderately, though he may succeed for a time, sooner or later the disease will be rekindled and he will be in trouble again. The job of the therapist is to recognize this inevitable recurrence and to aid his patient in accepting that fact. While the psychotherapy that achieves this may require penetration into the unconscious defiance of, hostility toward and rejection of reality, including the inability to drink normally, this tapping of unconscious activity cannot and does not resolve the disease, alcoholism. At best, it helps the patient to live with his limitation.

Summary

This communication has attempted primarily to enlist the interest of psychiatrists in the study of alcoholism. It was pointed out that neglect on the part of psychiatrists has sometimes produced a reaction of indifference to psychiatric help. It was suggested that study and investigation of the condition had been hampered by inadequate opportunities for close and prolonged contacts. It was also indicated that part of the failure to come to grips with alcoholism lay in faulty assumptions about the nature of the ailment. The concept of alcoholism as a runaway symptom was advanced. Support for this concept was derived, first, from the empirical fact that, once alcoholism has developed, a return to normal drinking is impossible; and secondly, from the results of the efforts of Alcoholics Anonymous, whose program of ignoring the issue of causation and focusing directly on the drinking itself brings that behavior to a complete halt in an impressive percentage of alcoholics.

Whether or not these considerations be held clarifying and in agreement with the facts, one primary point seems beyond challenge: that, as a group, psychiatrists have not made their weight sufficiently felt in the field of alcoholism. It is to be hoped that they will recognize their responsibility with respect to the problem and put forth the necessary time and effort to enable them to meet that responsibility with wisdom and a growing degree of firsthand knowledge.

The Act of Surrender in the Therapeutic Process, with Special Reference to Alcoholism[1]

Introduction: The Importance of a Positive Attitude

A year and a half ago, I wrote a paper in which I discussed a phenomenon that I labeled "conversion." In that paper I broadened the concept of conversion to cover any major switch from negative to positive thinking and feeling irrespective of a possible religious component. Two points stood out to me as important: first, the fact that the positive frame of mind could appear under a given set of circumstances without special help, psychiatric or otherwise; and second, that the new state of mind had a decidedly healthier tone to its thinking and feeling than that which prevailed when the negative tone was uppermost. Without specifically saying so, I then believed that the positive frame of mind could become a legitimate aim in therapy as, once it was brought about, the individual's attitudes and responses were much healthier.

While I no longer believe that therapy is simply a matter of reaching a positive relationship with reality, I remain convinced that the creation of a positive attitude is one of the essential features in a successful therapeutic program, and that any experience that brings about such an attitude or frame of mind deserves careful study for the light it may throw on treatment in general. Consequently, I continued my observations on the conversion experience and have arrived at the conclusion that the key to an understanding of that experience may be found in the act of surrender, which, in my opinion, sets in motion the conversion switch. My paper will therefore consist of (1) a discussion of the act of surrender, and (2) an endeavor to relate it to the therapeutic process as a whole.

Before I go ahead, it may be wise to recapitulate the contents of [a] previous paper. In it I described how, with the conversion switch, many aspects of the patient's attitudes underwent profound and often remarkable alterations. I pointed out how, in eight major ways, the individual switched or changed. Rather than go through the whole list again, I can sum up these changes briefly by saying that the person who has achieved the positive frame of mind has lost his or her tense, aggressive, demanding, conscience-ridden self that feels isolated and at odds with the world and has become a relaxed, natural, more realistic individual who can dwell in the world on a "live and let live" basis. The difference in the before and after state of these people is very real and represents, I believe, a fundamental psychic occurrence.

The Act of Surrender

With respect to the act of surrender, let me emphasize this point: It is an unconscious event, not willed by the patient even if he or she should desire to do so. It can occur only when an individual with certain traits in his or her unconscious mind becomes involved in a certain set of circumstances. Then the act of surrender can be anticipated with considerable accuracy, as I shall soon show. It cannot be defined in direct conscious terminology but must be understood in all its unconscious ramifications before its true inner meaning can be glimpsed.

The simplest way to picture what is involved in the act of surrender is to present a case in which there was a conversion experience that seemed to follow an act of surrender.

One Man's Story

The patient is a man in his early fifties, very successful in business, and referred to by his associates as Napoleon because of his autocratic methods when he was stirred up. For years, heavy drinking to the point of frequent intoxication was present, interfering to some extent with his efficiency, but never to the degree that his business really suffered. My first contact came some six or seven years ago when he came to Blythewood to dry out. Pursuant to our policy of trying slowly and from time to time to educate patients about the danger of their condition, we permitted this man to remain just for the drying out, at the same time telling him that, in our eyes, he was headed for trouble if he continued on his present trend. Without putting any pressure on him and thus arousing his resistance, we placed the facts before him and let it go at that.

We continued the policy of letting him come and go pretty much as he pleased, always, however, keeping uppermost before him the need to do something about his drinking, and always making it evident that we were not interested in drying him out, but in the real problem of helping him stop his drinking. Later on, and in retrospect, the patient, in referring to these tactics, said, "I used to like to come here; you didn't always argue with me. I always knew just where you stood and knew I wasn't fooling you any."

During all this time, however, I was working on his life situation so that ultimately it would provide the necessary dynamite to jar him loose from his whirl of self-centeredness. Gradually, his wife gave up her protectiveness and, before the time of this last admission nearly two years ago, she had determined to leave him if his drinking continued. Moreover, as a result of some discussion with me, his business partner had decided that he, with several key members of the firm, would tender their resignations if the patient did not make a real effort to mend his ways.

After a particularly severe bout, the patient was induced again to enter Blythewood. This time, however, I told him flatly that he would sign himself in for thirty days or he would go elsewhere; we were through with him running his case once and for all. He looked startled, picked up his hat, fiddled with it, and then put it on his head, saying, "Where's your pen? I'll go to Hilltop where I belong," referring to the cottage where he had dried out on previous occasions. Within three or four days he was off the liquor and thinking reasonably straight. He was then informed of his wife's decision and, instead of ranting around and making it clear where she could go, he discussed for the first time the real hell he had put her through and really seemed regretful. By the end of the first week, quite prepared for trouble, the partner told him of the pending resignations if the drinking persisted, only to be surprised and pleased with the patient's quiet acceptance of their decision and an acknowledgment of his own real wish to be different. He soon joined AA and is now an active member of that organization in his home community. The patient has to date stayed sober.

What Happened?

Recently in discussing his experience the man in the story explained, "You did something to me when you made me sign that card. I knew you meant business. I knew my wife was getting sore and that Bill [his partner] was fed up, but when you showed me you were through fooling, that was a clincher. I knew I needed help and couldn't get out of it myself. So I signed the card and felt better right off for doing it. I made up my mind that I wasn't going to run my own case any longer but was going to take orders. Then later I talked with Chris [his wife] and learned how she felt, and then Bill came along and I knew deep inside my heart they were right. But, I didn't mind. I didn't get angry and want to argue like I used to. I kind of surprised myself by agreeing with them. It sure was nice not to have to fight. I felt calmer and quieter inside and have ever since, although I know I'm not out of the woods yet."

Here is the story of a patient who has been through a conversion experience and is still in the positive phase. His own account of what happened stresses the signing of the card as the turning point in his experience, and I am also convinced that he is right. We can sum this man's experience up by saying that after trying to run his own case to his own ruination, he gave up the battle and surrendered to the need for help, after which he entered a new state of mind that has enabled him to remain sober.

Breaking Down the Act of Surrender

This man's experience, which is not limited to alcoholics, raises three questions:

1. What qualities were there in his nature that so long resisted help and finally were forced to give in?
2. What were the circumstances that brought about the final act of surrender?
3. Why does a positive phase follow the surrender experience?

My answers to these questions are derived primarily from my studies of alcoholics, but not entirely, as I have witnessed surrender with a typical aftermath in at least four cases among the students at Sarah Lawrence. I hope through my discussion in reply to these questions not only to define the act of surrender, but also to give you some feeling for it as a psychological entity or event.

Internal Qualities

To turn then to the first question, "What are the qualities in a patient's nature that make him or her put up such a battle before finally surrendering?" In the alcoholic, my observations have led me to see that the two qualities that Sillman selected as characteristic—*defiant individuality* and *grandiosity*—may very well explain that the alcoholic is typically resistant to the point of being unreasonable and stubborn about seeking help or being able to accept help even when he or she seeks it. Defiant individuality and grandiosity operate in the unconscious layers of the mind, and their influence must be understood if one is to see what probably goes on at the time of surrender.

Defiance

Defiance may be defined as a quality that permits an individual to snap his fingers in the face of reality and live on unperturbed. It has two special values for handling life situations. In the first place, defiance, certainly with alcoholics, is a surprisingly effective tool for managing anxiety or reality, both of which are so often a source of anxiety. If you defy a fact and say it is not so and can succeed in doing so unconsciously, you can drink to the day of your death, forever denying the imminence of that fate. As one patient phrased it, "My defiance was a cloak of armor." And so it was a most trustworthy shield against the truth and all its pressures.

In the second place, defiance masquerades as a very real and reliable source of inner strength and self-confidence, since it says in essence, "Nothing can happen to me because I can and do defy it." With people who meet reality on this basis, life is always a battle, with the spoils going to the strong. Much can be said in favor of defiance as a method of meeting life. It is the main resource of the chin-up and unafraid type of adjustment and, as a temporary measure, it helps people over many rough spots.

Grandiosity

Grandiosity, the second quality noted by Sillman, permeates widely throughout the reactions of the alcoholic. Differing from defiance—which seems almost uniquely structuralized in the psyche of the alcoholic—grandiosity springs from the persisting infantile ego. As in other neurotic states, grandiosity characteristically fills a person with feelings of omnipotence, demands for direct gratification of wishes, and a proneness to interpret frustration as evidence of rejection and lack of love. The effect of this persistence in the alcoholic is not a bit different from the effect of any other neurotic. Perhaps in the alcoholic the typical arrogance and sense of superior worth are kept nearer the surface by the associated defiance that feeds the childish ego constantly by its succession of victories. By and large, however, there is nothing in the alcoholic's grandiosity that distinguishes him or her from the neurotic, whose infantile ego survives to become a significant factor in adult life; it is part of the typical egocentricity of that group, and its presence is confirmed by any careful study of them.

Defiance and Grandiosity at Work in the Alcoholic

We are now in a position to discuss how these qualities operate in alcoholics. On the one side, the defiance says, "It is not true that I can't manage drinking." On the other side, the facts speak loudly and with increasing insistence to the contrary. Again, on the one side, grandiosity claims, "There is nothing I cannot master and control." And, on the other side, the facts demonstrate unmistakably the opposite. The dilemma of the alcoholic is now obvious: the unconscious mind rejects—through its capacity for defiance and grandiosity—what the conscious mind perceives. Hence, realistically, the individual is frightened by his or her drinking and at the same time is prevented from doing anything about it by the unconscious activity that can and does ignore or override the conscious mind.

Let us see how this clash between the conscious and unconscious response manifests itself in the clinical setting. A stimulus from reality, such as a recognition of the downhill pattern of the drinking, impinges upon the conscious mind and creates acute anxiety that, for the moment, dominates the conscious processes and is recorded as worry, distress, fear, and concern. The patient, in this state, is filled with a desire to quit and eagerly grabs at any kind of help. He or she is in a state of crisis and suffering.

In the meantime, however, the stimulus of reality is hitting the unconscious layers of the mind and is stirring up the reactions of defiance and grandiosity. Since, characteristically, it takes a certain amount of time before the unconscious responses are sufficiently mobilized to influence conscious mental activity, there is always an appreciable lag before the conscious mind evidences signs of the underlying unconscious activity. Then slowly and gradually these attitudes supervene. Patients express less concern about their drinking, complain that they were rushed into seeking help, that they're no worse than anybody else, and that the worry of others is silly and a gratuitous invasion of their rights. Finally, the memory of their own acute period of anxiety is swallowed up by the defiance and grandiosity. Thus the patient loses the effectiveness of the anxiety as a stimulus to create suffering and a desire for change. This cycle will go on repeating itself as long as the defiance and the grandiosity continue to function with unimpaired vigor.

External Circumstances

We now come to the second question, "What were the circumstances that made that patient give in and sign that card?" Let me review them for you briefly. He had been drinking for years, and he knew his drinking was getting worse in the eyes of family and friends. However, he knew that his condition had reached the point where both his wife and his business associates were leaving him and thereby withdrawing their support and protection. He was threatened with the task of managing himself and his condition entirely on his own, so he sought my help and protection to dry him out and thus allow him once more to resume his role of successful defiance and grandiosity. This time, however, I refused to follow my previous role. I had established myself as not arbitrary, not willing to fit what he needed. But when I asked him to sign the card, I knew that his other circumstances were different and that I represented the one way for him. When I told him, in essence, that he was not running his case or me anymore, his last prop was thus removed. He had no place to take his defiance and his grandiosity; nor could he become defiant with me: someone who stood for his last bit of hope and who actually had become established as an ultimate resource when he was in difficulty. So he staged a brief inward debate and then signed the card. The act of surrender had occurred.

In short, the patient signed the card, first, when all support was withdrawn; second, when he could not in anger defy those who withdrew their support because he knew they had been patient and long-suffering; and third, when he found himself desperately needing help and had no grandiose ideas left about being able to drink like nonalcoholics. He had neither unconscious defiance nor grandiosity left to fight with. He was licked, and he both knew it and felt it.

The Positive Phase

We now reach the third question, "Why does the positive phase follow?" Here, we frankly reach speculation. I know the positive phase comes, but not just why. Surrender means cessation of a fight, and cessation of a fight seems logically to be followed by internal peace and quiet. That point seems fairly obvious, but why the whole feeling tone switches from negative to positive without all the concomitant changes is not so clear. Nevertheless, despite my inability to explain the phenomenon, there is no question that the changes do take place and that they may be initiated by an act of surrender.

The Difference between Submission and Surrender

One fact must be kept in mind, namely, the need to distinguish between submission and surrender. In submission, an individual accepts reality consciously, but not unconsciously. He or she accepts as a practical fact that he or she cannot at that moment lick reality, but lurking in the unconscious is the feeling, "There'll come a day," which implies no real acceptance and demonstrates conclusively that the struggle is still on. With submission, which at best is a superficial yielding, tension continues.

When an individual surrenders, the ability to accept reality functions on the unconscious level, and there is no residual of battle; relaxation with freedom from strain and conflict ensues. In fact, it is perfectly possible to ascertain how much acceptance of reality is on the unconscious level by the degree of relaxation that develops. The greater the relaxation, the greater the inner acceptance of reality.

We can now be more precise in our definition of an act of surrender. *It is to be viewed as a moment when the unconscious forces of defiance and grandiosity actually cease to function effectively.* When that happens, the individual is wide open to reality; he or she can listen and learn without conflict and fighting back. He or she is receptive to life, not antagonistic. The person senses a feeling of relatedness and at-oneness that becomes the source of an inner peace and serenity, the possession of which frees the individual from the compulsion to drink. In other words, an act of surrender is an occasion wherein the individual no longer fights life, but accepts it.

Having defined an act of surrender as a moment of accepting reality on the unconscious level, it is now possible to define the emotional state of surrender as *a state in which there is a persisting capacity to accept reality*. In this definition, the capacity to accept reality must not be conceived of in a passive sense, but in the active sense of reality being a place where one can live and function as a person acknowledging one's responsibilities and feeling free to make that reality more livable for oneself and others. There is no sense of "must"; nor is there any sense of fatalism. With true unconscious surrender, the acceptance of reality means the individual can work in it and with it. The state of surrender is really positive and creative.

To sum up, my observations have led me to conclude that an act of surrender is inevitably followed by a state of surrender that is actually the positive state in the conversion picture. Because of the two always being associated, I believe they represent a single phenomenon, to which I attach the term *surrender reaction*.

Relating the Act of Surrender to the Therapeutic Process

Having at last made as clear as I could my use of the term *surrender*, I must now try to relate that concept to the therapeutic process. While a recognition of the dynamic force of the event has proven enlightening in many directions, it has been particularly helpful in understanding the fluctuations in moods of patients and in certain aspects of therapy.

The following patient's problem took on meaning for me when I grasped the fact that he had experienced an act of surrender at the time he attended his first AA meeting. A man in his middle thirties, he tells his story this way:

"I was licked. I'd tried everything, and nothing had worked. My wife was packing to leave me; my job was going to blow up in my face. I was desperate when I went to my first AA meeting. When I got there, something happened. I don't know to this day [a year later] what it was, but I took a look at the men and women there and I knew they had something I needed, so I said to myself, 'I'll listen to what they have to tell me.' From that time on, things have been different. I go to meetings, work with other drunks, and study all I can about alcoholism. I know I'm an alcoholic, and I never let that fact escape me."

Now, if you stop and review this man's account, you will note the statement, "I'll listen to what they have to tell me." In that comment to himself, the patient initiated his act of surrender.

There was no lip service in his willingness to listen; he really wanted help. There was no defiance or grandiosity available at the moment to dilute his listening. He was accepting, without inner reservation or conflict, the reality of his condition and the need for help. And, significantly enough, at this point he goes on to say, "From that time on, things have been different." Subsequent events clearly indicate that this man did experience the typical change I have been calling *conversion,* and from that time on "things were different." His wife, commenting on this change, said feelingly, "It's the most remarkable thing I ever could imagine. The only trouble is that I still have to keep my fingers crossed because it still doesn't make any sense to me."

The patient, however, consulted me because he "didn't like the way things were going." By that, he meant that he was finding himself cranky at home and irritable in business, signs that his AA experience had taught him were ominous. When I asked him why he gave up drinking, he replied that he had made up his mind to quit so he did, although he had to admit that AA was helpful. A little surprised at this simple assertion and doubting it somewhat, I plied him with further questions and got the real story, which showed to me that he had a typical surrender experience, followed by a typical positive aftermath. But I also saw that the change did not last and that, after several months in which the patient had lived in a state of surrender, he slowly reverted to his former attitudes and ways of feeling. In other words, the surrender reaction did not fix itself into his personality and thus allowed the return of his previous state of mind.

Differing Acts of Surrender

The fate of the surrender reaction is in itself an interesting study. With some, the surrender experience is the start of genuine growth and maturation. With others, the surrender phase is the only one ever reached, so that they never lose the need to attend meetings and to follow the program assiduously, apparently relying on the constant reminders in their daily existence to supply the necessary impetus to the surrender feeling, at least insofar as alcohol is concerned. For a few, there seems to occur a phenomenon of what might be called selective surrender. After the effects of the initial surrender experience have worn away, the individual returns to pretty much the same person he or she was before, except for the fact that the person doesn't drink. His surrender is not to life as a person, but to alcohol as an alcoholic. Many other differing aftermaths undoubtedly occur, but a study of any or all of them would, I am sure, disclose the same basic fact: The surrender experience is followed by a phase of positive thinking and feeling that undergoes various vicissitudes before it becomes established in some form or other in the psyche—or it is lost completely, becoming merely a memory and a mirage.

Recognizing the Surrender Reaction

From the standpoint of therapy, recognition of the surrender reaction throws a challenging light upon many clinical phenomena that are generally held to be of significance in the process of getting better. For instance, in catharsis it is not what is revealed but the act of surrender (that preceded and permitted the revealing to come to light) that, in my opinion, produces the characteristic afterglow of positive feeling. It also explains its temporary effect just as with the conversion experience of the alcoholic. Again, the frequent unexpected lifts derived from seemingly ordinary first interviews, while they may be considered transference phenomena, seem to me more in the nature of "surrender reactions" based upon the fact that the client found the interview palatable, and the client made a decision to continue, which by implication means "surrender" to the psychiatrist. The very decision to come to a psychiatrist, through its surrender significance, often has an ameliorating influence and certainly accounts for the remark of a patient who said, "Once I rang your doorbell, I felt 75 percent better." The phenomenon of release, which makes people realize that, in losing their lives they are finding them, becomes explicable if one sees that the surrender that preceded the sense of release stills the inner fight and hostility, thus permitting the spontaneous creative elements of the Inner Self outlet for expression.

Resistance

It is in the area of resistance, however, that an understanding of the surrender reaction sheds the greatest light on the therapeutic process. Regularly, therapy goes ahead by fits and starts. For a while there is a period of resistance that is worked through, permitting progress, insight, and awareness of the emotional interplays in the unconscious life. Then another point of resistance is encountered, and again it must be ferreted out and dissolved before further constructive steps may be taken. Meeting resistance and working it through are the everyday tasks of therapy and familiar to you all.

Breaking through Resistance

Where before the patient has been in full resistance—bucking treatment, difficult to manage, getting nowhere—suddenly there is a marked change, almost like the sun bursting through the clouds, bringing everything into focus and making what was once a confused jumble take on form, significance, and meaning. For the time being, the resistances have disappeared and the treatment proceeds apace.

We have been accustomed to saying that the patient has a flash of insight and understanding that brought clarification and a greater awareness of his or her individual emotional makeup. Actually, if you examine the state of mind that breaks through when the resistance melts, you will find it is strikingly parallel to the positive state of mind an individual may have after a conversion experience. In fact, the parallel is so striking that I am more and more becoming convinced that the two are identical. In other words, I now believe that the giving up of resistance during treatment is in reality an act of surrender that typically, as in the conversion experience, is followed by a positive state of mind where elements of resistance are no longer present. This "giving in" may be sudden, causing the patient to enter the positive phase so rapidly as to constitute a sudden turnover with dramatic results. Generally, as in the conversion change, the change is slower, but the alteration is in exactly the same direction.

Conclusion

No one recognizes more than I do the sweeping nature of any such observations. No one is more aware than I am of the need to substantiate these observations with clinical material. Someday I may be able to support more conclusively my present hypothesis with case material. I can point out, however, that the positive aftermath of the so-called successful interpretation is no more lasting than the positive phase of the so-called conversion experience. They are both temporary; they are both slowly supplanted by a new crop of resistances or negative feelings. Also, they both require further change in the unconscious mind before the act of surrender becomes a settled state of surrender in which defiance and grandiosity no longer raise havoc with adjustment, serenity, and the capacity to function as a human being.

To recapitulate, my studies of the conversion experience have led me to see that

- it is the act of surrender that initiates the switch from negative to positive behavior
- it occurs when the unconscious defiance and grandiosity are for the time being rendered completely powerless by force of circumstance or reality
- the act of surrender and the change that follows are inseparable since it is safe to assume that if there is no change, there has been no surrender
- the positive phase is really a state of surrender that follows the act of surrender
- in several places, as in catharsis, the so-called improvement or feeling better is actually a state of surrender induced by an act of surrender
- the state of surrender, if maintained, supplies an emotional tone to all thinking and feeling that does ensure healthy adjustment

I have tried in this paper to establish the fact that there is such a psychic event as surrender and that once the fact is appreciated in all its ramifications, it is illuminating clinically and provides a basis for understanding much that goes on in the therapeutic process.

Surrender versus Compliance in Therapy, with Special Reference to Alcoholism[1]

Since becoming a sideline observer of Alcoholics Anonymous in 1939, my approach to alcoholism has undergone an almost total reorientation. For the first time I saw what peace of mind means in the achievement of sobriety, and I began to consider the emotional factors involved from a very different viewpoint. In AA meetings, the role of resentments was a recurrent theme. This seemed significant. Continuing this line of observation, I found that another enemy of sobriety was defiance, which Sillman[2] had already described as "defiant individuality," a major hallmark of the personality of alcoholics.

Another significant emphasis in AA was humility and "hitting bottom," completely new points of emphasis for me. It was clear that if the individual remained stiff-necked, he would continue to drink, but I could not see why. Finally the presence of an apparently unconquerable ego became evident. It was this ego that had to become humble. Then the role of hitting bottom, which means reaching a feeling of personal helplessness, began to be clear. It was this process that produced in the ego an awareness of vulnerability, initiating the positive phase. In hitting bottom the ego becomes tractable and is ready for humility. The conversion experience[3] has started.

What happens in the unconscious at the time of hitting bottom remained a mystery. The first elucidation came from a patient. Through psychotherapy she was gradually losing the intractable ego structure and finally, for rather obscure reasons, she had a minor conversion experience that brought her relative peace and quiet. During this phase she began attending various churches in town. One Monday morning she entered the office, her eyes shining, and said at once, "I know what happened to me. I heard it in a hymn yesterday. I surrendered when I had that experience." Guided by this clue, I realize that hitting bottom is ineffectual if not followed by a surrender. Hitting bottom must produce a result, and this result is surrender.

Most of my ideas along these lines were incorporated in an article[4] on "the act of surrender" in relation to the therapeutic process. I now wish to extend these thoughts a step further. The surrender concept has not generally been well received except by some AA's who recognize its validity in their own experiences. One or two psychiatrists have told me they are beginning to see the usefulness of the concept but no one, to my knowledge, has yet come forward with a paper supporting the thesis of surrender out of his own observations.

One reason for this lag is the resistance to the idea of surrender. It seems too completely defeatist. Were I writing that article now, I would change it in this respect so as to discuss the term *surrender* in linkage with other, less-to-be-shunned concepts. But those links were discovered only later.

In the article on surrender, I said:

> One fact must be kept in mind, namely the need to distinguish between submission and surrender. In submission, an individual accepts reality consciously but not unconsciously. He accepts as a practical fact that he cannot at that moment conquer reality, but lurking in his unconscious is the feeling, "There'll

come a day"—which implies no real acceptance and demonstrates conclusively that the struggle is still going on. With submission, which at best is a superficial yielding, tension continues. When, on the other hand, the ability to accept reality functions on the unconscious level, there is no residual of battle, and relaxation ensues with freedom from strain and conflict. In fact, it is perfectly possible to ascertain to what extent the acceptance of reality is on the unconscious level by the degree of relaxation which develops. The greater the relaxation, the greater the inner acceptance of reality.

Understanding Acceptance

In that paragraph the words *accept* and *acceptance* are each used three times. I saw at the time that surrender leads to acceptance. What I failed to see and emphasize was the very important relationship between surrender and the capacity for acceptance.

I propose, therefore, first, to consider acceptance as a human capacity, and second, to discuss the blocks to the development of acceptance. The importance of acceptance is widely recognized although often only by indirection. Sometimes the necessity for acceptance is bluntly stated, as in Grayson's recent article on the role of "acceptance" in physical rehabilitation.[5] Grayson reports his discovery that the individual who needs rehabilitation remains a poor prospect until he finally accepts his need for the rehabilitating procedures. More often the concept of acceptance is dragged in by the heels with little or no recognition that acceptance itself is a major psychological step. Two recent illustrations are worthy of mention. In a summarizing article on Alcoholics Anonymous, in the *Connecticut Review on Alcoholism*,[6] the following statements appear: "He does not have to fight against ideas which come from this group, he can accept them. Thus the idea that he is an alcoholic is acceptable when coming from this group. The need to avoid the 'first drink' is accepted." Certainly the need for acceptance is unequivocally stated. And the following statement is from Kubie's book: "The man who is normal can accept the guidance of reason, reality and commonsense."[7] The word *accept* is scattered throughout the pages of the book, but the question of acceptance is never raised—as if it were something that needs no discussion.

The first of the Alcoholics Anonymous Twelve Steps reads: "We admitted we were powerless over alcohol—that our lives had become unmanageable." The second word is *admitted,* which in many ways is a blood brother of *acceptance,* although many an AA meeting has been devoted to quibbling about the difference between *admit* and *accept.* Time and again slips are explained on the basis that the one who slips has not truly accepted his alcoholism.

The word *accept,* thus, appears quite regularly in speech and writing, but never is there much discussion of how acceptance comes about. The usual explanation is that, if the doctor is accepting, the patient will be so too; in case of failure, the therapist is held responsible, just as parents are for their children. To suppose that acceptance is caught by contagion is a pretty thought. It is not, however, likely to stimulate much understanding of individual psychodynamics. It is not enough merely to point the finger elsewhere.

There is need, therefore, to discuss the dynamics of acceptance in the individual. Acceptance appears to be a state of mind in which the individual accepts rather than rejects or resists: He is able to take things in, to go along with, to cooperate, to be receptive. Contrariwise, he is not argumentative, quarrelsome, irritable, or contentious. For the time being, at any rate, the hostile, negative, aggressive elements are in abeyance, and we have a much pleasanter human being to deal with. Acceptance as a state of mind has many highly admirable qualities as well as useful ones. Some measure of it is greatly to be desired. Its attainment as an inner state of mind is never easy.

It is necessary to point out that no one can tell himself or force himself wholeheartedly to accept anything. One must have a *feeling—conviction—*otherwise the acceptance is not wholehearted but halfhearted with a large element of lip service. There is a string of words that describe halfhearted acceptance: *submission, resignation, yielding, compliance, acknowledgment, concession,* and so forth. With each of these words there is a feeling of reservation, a tug in the direction of nonacceptance.

Most people regard nonacceptance as a sign of willful refusal; this bypasses all current knowledge of the unconscious elements in resistance and willpower. Others, better informed about those attributes, avoid the use of such a phrase as *willful refusal.* They know that it is largely unconscious attitudes and feelings that determine the conscious thinking and hence do not suppose that resistance can be given up by an act of will on the part of the conscious mind.

Acceptance: A Step beyond Recognition

Those who recognize the role of unconscious forces then take a curious next step: They talk about undermining the resistance by uncovering the reasons for the particular series of resistance, as if the unconscious mind must then accept those reasons—a non sequitur. It is one thing to see reasons and quite another thing to behave with corresponding rationality. One patient neatly punctured this assumption. After eight years of analysis with four therapists of different schools, he began to get some inkling of acceptance as a state of mind that he sadly lacked. Finally, in a burst of awareness, he remarked, "I know all the reasons but I don't know how to be reasonable." That statement aptly summed up his predicament. His logical mind could perceive and believe all the factors underlying his difficulties, but he remained cantankerous and unreasonable as far as his feeling life was concerned. In his head, or conscious mind, he could "accept" the explanations, but deep inside where the heart, or the unconscious, operates there was no feeling of acceptance. That capacity still had to be developed. Uncovering reasons for behavior, no matter how convincing, does not and cannot ensure acceptance of those reasons. Acceptance is a step beyond recognition, a further operation in the process of therapy. Many therapists have failed to discern this two-stage process. The clue was my patient's use of the word *reasonable*. He could have said, with accuracy, "reasonable and accepting," because he was beginning to appreciate the fact that one's frame of mind governs one's response to things that are reasonable or, for that matter, unreasonable.

What was not clearly appreciated is the fact that a state of reasonableness or acceptance or receptivity has an emotional origin that rises from exactly the same source as does the resistance and the forces that predominantly contribute to our being willing, namely, the unconscious. Unless the unconscious has within it the capacity to accept, the conscious mind can only tell itself that it should accept, but by so doing it cannot bring about acceptance in the unconscious, which continues with its own non-accepting and resenting attitudes. The result is a house divided against itself: The conscious mind sees all the reasons for acceptance while the unconscious mind says, "But I *won't* accept!" Wholehearted acceptance under such conditions is impossible. Experience has proved that in the alcoholic a halfhearted reaction does not maintain sobriety for very long. The inner doubts all too soon take over. The alcoholic who stays "dry" must be wholehearted. Here we meet a complication. People accept the necessity of being wholehearted about alcoholism but not about everything else. They are determined to maintain their capacity for resistance. They fear the fact that if they become total acceptors they will have no ability whatsoever to resist and will become "pushovers," complete "Caspar Milquetoasts."

Such fears of passivity are supported not only by conscious logic but also by deep unconscious sources that cannot be dealt with in the present paper. Powerful forces are aligned against acceptance, producing in the individual extreme conflict, which must be resolved if the capacity for acceptance is ever to develop.

Compliance: Partial Surrender

We are thus confronted with the question: "What does produce wholehearted acceptance?" My answer is, as before, surrender. But surrender is a step not easily taken by human beings. In recent years, because of my special interest in the phenomenon of surrender, I have become aware of another conscious and unconscious phenomenon, namely, compliance—which is basically partial acceptance or partial surrender, and which often serves as a block to surrender. The remainder of this paper will concern itself with that reaction and how it throws light on the handling of patients, particularly alcoholics.

Compliance needs careful definition. It means agreeing,

going along, but in no way implies enthusiastic, whole-hearted assent and approval. There is a willingness not to argue or resist, but the cooperation is a bit grudging, a little forced; one is not entirely happy about agreeing. *Compliance* is, therefore, a word that portrays mixed feelings, divided sentiments. There is a willingness to go along but at the same time there are some inner reservations which make that willingness somewhat thin and watery. It does not take much to overthrow this kind of willingness. The existence of this attitude will probably appear as neither strange nor new. Nor is it, until one begins to see how it operates in the unconscious.

One thing must be made absolutely clear: There is a world of difference between thinking of compliance in conscious terms and in unconscious terms. The following discussion is focused wholly on unconscious reactions and cannot be translated into conscious reactions until the possible effect of the former upon the latter is appreciated. An illustration at this point may be helpful. An alcoholic, at the termination of a long and painful spree, decides that he has had enough. This decision is announced loudly and vehemently to all who will listen. His sincerity cannot be questioned. He means every word of it. Yet he knows, and so do those who hear him, that he will be singing another tune before many weeks have elapsed. For the moment he seems to have accepted his alcoholism, but it is only with a skin-deep assurance. He will certainly revert to drinking. What we see here is compliance in action. During the time when his memory of the suffering entailed by a spree is acute and painful he agrees to anything and everything. But deep inside, in his unconscious, the best he can do is to comply—which means that, when the reality of his drinking problem becomes undeniable, he no longer argues with incontrovertible facts. The fight, so to speak, has been knocked out of him. As time passes and the memory of his suffering weakens, the need for compliance lessens. As the need diminishes, the half of compliance that never really accepted begins to stir once more and soon resumes its sway. The need for accepting the illness of alcoholism is ignored because, after all, deep inside he really did not mean it, he had only complied. Of course, consciously the victim of all this is completely in the dark. What he gets is messages from below that slowly bring about a change in his conscious attitudes. For a while drink was anathema, but now he begins to toy with the thought of one drink, and so on, until finally, as the noncooperative element in compliance takes over, he has his first drink. The other half of compliance has won out; the alcoholic is the unwitting victim of his unconscious inclinations.

It is the nature of the word to have this two-faced quality of agreeing and then reneging. It is only by realizing the widespread ramifications of the compliance tendency that its far-flung importance can be appreciated.

One of the first things to recognize is the fact that the presence of compliance blocks the capacity for true acceptance. Since compliance is a form of acceptance, every time the individual is faced with the need to accept something, he falls back on compliance, which serves for the moment—the individual consciously believing that he has accepted. But since he has no real capacity to accept, he is soon swinging in the other direction, his seeming acceptance a thing of the past. In other words, the best an inwardly complying person can do toward acceptance is to comply. During treatment the patient regularly is surprised to learn that his previous tendency to agree in order to be agreeable was merely a lot of compliance without any genuine capacity to accept.

This unconscious split in the compliance mechanism has deep psychosomatic reverberations. One patient, who had uncovered a wide streak of compliance, had a dream in which he placed the two components of compliance side by side, disclosing their utter incompatibility. What he saw was that his wish to be cooperative and well liked while yet maintaining his ego intact meant certain conflict with other people whose very existence was a threat to his own ego. He was torn by the dilemma of being nice and pleasant or being a man and holding his own. His next dream contained a busy ferryboat plying back and forth across a river. As the patient watched, it went faster and faster and faster, the patient following its motion closely. Soon it seemed as if he were following the flight of a tennis ball while sitting at the net, his head turning more and more rapidly until finally he became giddy and woke up feeling dizzy. When the patient, a physician, saw the connection between this dream and the dilemma of his preceding dream, he laughed and remarked, "You know, I have been doctoring for many years and have heard all about this psychosomatic business, but I never thought I would learn about it from myself."

Compliance creates other problems for the individual. Since it says yes on the surface and no inside, it contributes to the sense of guilt. The person who says yes and feels the opposite has an inward realization that he is a two-faced liar; this stirs up his conscience and evokes a feeling of guilt. Compliance also adds mightily to the problems of inferiority. The guilt reaction increases the sense of inferiority, but the compliance response engrafts it even more. The unconscious situation can be outlined thus: Compliance is a form of agreeing, of never stand-ing up for oneself. When that response is automatic, rou-tine, and unvarying, the individual gets a feeling that he cannot stand up for himself; this inevitably augments his inferiority problems.

Compliance and Alcoholism

It is now possible to link compliance with the problem of alcoholism and also to the theory of surrender. The link between alcoholism and compliance has already been shown in the alcoholic's repeated vows that he would never take another drink, vows that go by the board be-cause of the inner inability to do more than comply. The presence of a strong vein of unconscious compliance in the alcoholic can be demonstrated in other ways. Alco-holics are a notably pleasant and agreeable group with a marked tendency to say yes when approached directly. They claim they want to be well liked—hence their will-ingness to promise anything. Yet—and here the other side of the compliance reaction is manifest—they balk at the showdown and are ever likely to renege on their original promises. As another illustration, they are keen to go to a show, buy tickets in advance, and then on the night of the performance wish they had never had the idea. Characteristically, one man always calls up at the last moment for a date, knowing that if he had made the en-gagement in advance his present wish would later appear as a "must" that he had to live up to. He, like so many of his kind, has to do things on the spur of the moment. Otherwise, the contrary half gets into action and the proj-ect is opposed and quashed. A favorite remark, "Let's have some fun," must mean immediately: the desire evap-orates if there is any planning to be done. Often alco-holics go downtown merely looking for fun with not a thought of a drink on their minds—in fact, quite "compliant" to the need for sobriety. When they find the fun, however, the chances are that they will be in trouble before the night is over. Undoubtedly the initial restlessness that stimulated the need for some fun had its origin in the early rumblings of the noncompliance elements. Much of the apparent dual personality of alcoholics becomes understandable if their behavior is seen in the light of conflicting trends.

The next point, the relationship between compliance and surrender, has already been intimated in the remark that compliance blocks the capacity to surrender. The inability to surrender may seem a small loss until the matter is studied more thoughtfully.

After an act of surrender, the individual reports a sense of unity, of ended struggles, of no longer divided inner counsel. He knows the meaning of inner wholeness and, what is more, he knows from immediate experience the feeling of being wholehearted about anything. He recognizes for the first time how insincere his previous protestations actually were. If he is a member of Alcoholics Anonymous, he travels around to meetings proclaiming the need for honesty—usually, at the start of his pilgrimage, with a certain amount of surprise and wonder in his voice. Quite frankly, before he was able to embrace the program, he had no idea he was a liar, dishonest in his thoughts; but now that AA is making sense—that is, he is accepting AA wholeheartedly and without reservations— he sees that previously he had never truly accepted anything. The AA speaker does not follow through to state that, formerly, all he had been doing was complying; but if asked, he nods his head in vigorous assent, saying, "That's exactly what I was doing." A more articulate individual, after a little thought, added: "You know, when I think back on it, that was all I knew how to do. I supposed that was the way it was with everybody. I could not conceive of really giving up. The best I could do was comply, which meant I never really wanted to quit drinking, down inside. I can see it all now but I certainly couldn't then."

Obviously this speaker is reporting the loss of his compliant tendencies, occurring, let it be noted, when he gave up, surrendered, and thus was able wholeheartedly to follow the AA program. Let it further be noted that this new honesty arises automatically, spontaneously; the individual does not have the slightest inkling that this development is in prospect. It represents a deep unconscious shift in attitude and one certainly for the better.

It is now possible to see the usurping, dog-in-the-manger role of compliance. As long as compliance is functioning, there is halfway but never total surrender. But the halfway surrender and acceptance, serving as it does to quell the fighting temporarily, deceives both the individual and the onlooker, neither of whom is able to detect the unconscious compliance in the reaction of apparent yielding. It is only when a real surrender occurs that compliance is knocked out of the picture, freeing the individual for a series of wholehearted responses—including, in the alcoholic, his acceptance of his illness and of his need to do something constructive about it.

Enough has been said, it would seem, to show the significance and the importance of understanding the relationship between compliance and the ability to surrender and accept. They are in complete opposition. As long as the former controls reactions, there can be no wholehearted acceptance, only the halfhearted kind, which is admittedly not sufficient. Results of real value can only come about when the compliant reactions have been successfully dissipated.

No Easy Road to Understanding

Some will ask how this can be brought about. The answer, insofar as I have been able to formulate it, is long, involved, and rather hazy. Experience shows that through psychotherapy the dominance of compliance over the unconscious can slowly be superseded, and that through the AA experience compliance can be temporarily and sometimes permanently blotted out. There does not appear to be any easy road to real understanding of this problem.

The preceding materials can now be summed up. It was pointed out that in an earlier article on the phenomenon of surrender, the tie of surrender to acceptance had not been sufficiently stressed. It was also pointed out that the concept of acceptance is freely talked about but rarely if ever made an object of study. Some observations regarding the nature of acceptance were reported and it was shown to contain two possible reactions, which we called wholehearted acceptance and halfhearted. It was then demonstrated how halfheartedness and compliance were closely allied. The nature of compliance was next discussed and, lastly, the antipathetic relationship between compliance on the one hand and surrender and acceptance on the other.

This is a long and rather circuitous route to the point of this paper, namely, that surrender is essential to wholehearted acceptance, and that unconscious compliance, which is a halfway surrender, can be a vital block to genuine surrender. It was then pointed out that alcoholics frequently show marked unconscious compliant trends, which not only help to explain some puzzling aspects of their behavior but also account for their frequent inability to respond meaningfully to treatment. Since the presence of these trends has been more clearly recognized, the response of many patients to therapy has been considerably more satisfactory. These considerations have been presented in the hope that others also may find that a recognition of the processes of surrender, acceptance, and compliance can be a source of help in tackling the alcoholic psychotherapeutically.

The Ego Factors
in Surrender in Alcoholism[1]

In the past fifteen years, my understanding of the nature of alcoholism as a disease has been influenced largely by insight into the mechanisms at work in the Alcoholics Anonymous process. Some years ago I stated that AA, to succeed, must induce a surrender on the part of the individual.[2] More recently, I discussed the idea of compliance[3] acting as a barrier to that real acceptance that a surrender produces. On this occasion I propose to extend my observations by discussing (a) what factors in the individual must surrender, and (b) how the surrender reaction changes the inner psychic picture.

The first question, what factors in the individual must surrender, received passing attention in the article on compliance. There, relative to the difficulty of surrender, I noted that "the presence of an apparently unconquerable ego became evident. It was this ego that had to become humble." The first part of the present communication will be devoted to an elaboration of the nature of this ego factor.

Use of the word *ego* involves always the possibility of confusion of meaning. For a time, therefore, I considered a substitute term. That idea was set aside because, despite possible misinterpretation, the word *ego* is current in everyday language in exactly the sense in which it will be employed in this discussion. The expression "he has an inflated ego" is self-explanatory. It evokes the picture of a pompous, self-important, strutting individual whose inferiorities are masked by a surface assurance. Such a person appears thick-skinned, insensitive, nearly impervious to the existence of others, a completely self-centered individual who plows unthinkingly through life, intent on gathering unto himself all the comforts and satisfactions available. He is generally considered the epitome of selfishness, and there the matter rests.

This popular view of ego, while it may not have scientific foundation, has one decided value: It possesses a meaning and can convey a concept that the average person can grasp. This concept of the inflated ego recognizes the common ancestor of a whole series of traits, namely, that they are all manifestations of an underlying feeling state in which personal considerations are first and foremost.

The existence of this ego has long been recognized, but a difficulty in terminology still remains. Part of the difficulty arises from the use of the word *ego,* in psychiatric and psychological circles, to designate those elements of the psyche that are supposed to rule psychic life. Freud divided mental life into three major subdivisions: the id, the ego, and the superego. The first, he stated, contains the feeling of life on a deep, instinctual level; the third is occupied by the conscience, whose function is to put brakes on the impulses arising within the id. The ego should act as mediator between the demands of the id and the restraints of the superego, which might be overzealous and bigoted. Freud's own research was concerned mainly with the activities of the id and the superego. The void he left with respect to the ego is one that his followers are endeavoring to fill, but as yet with no generally accepted conclusions.

Ego: Two Definitions

The word *ego*, however, has been preempted by the psychiatrists and psychologists, although they do not always agree among themselves about the meaning to be attached to it. The resulting confusion is the more lamentable because almost everyone, layman or scientist, would agree on the concept of the inflated ego. It would be helpful if other terms were found for the ego concepts about which there are differing views.

The solution for this dilemma will be to indicate with a capital *E* the big Ego, and without a capital to identify the personality aspect that Freud had in mind when he placed ego between id and superego.[4]

With this disposition of the problem of terminology, it is now possible to consider the first issue, namely, the Ego factors in the alcoholic that, through surrender, become humble. The concept of the enlarged Ego, as noted previously, is available to common observation. Those who do not recognize it in themselves can always see it in some member of their family or among friends and acquaintances—not to mention patients. Everyone knows egotistical people and has a perfectly clear idea of what the word means. Besides *egotistical*, and the series of words mentioned earlier, adjectives that help to round out the portrait of the egotistical person are *prideful, arrogant, pushing, dominating, attention-seeking, aggressive, opinionated, headstrong, stubborn, determined,* and *impatient.*

All these terms are inadequate, however, because they describe only surface features without conveying any feeling of the inner essence from which the Ego springs. Unless some appreciation for the source of the Ego is gained, the dynamic import is lost and the term may seem merely a form of name-calling. It is easy to say someone has a big Ego without awareness of what is really happening in the deep layers of that person's mind, without perception of the Ego. Nor is it a matter of intellect. The need here is to lay hold of the inner feeling elements upon which the activity of the Ego rests. Only when these elements become clear can the fundamental basis of the Ego also be clarified.

It is convenient, for the exposition of this inner functioning, to reverse the usual sequence and to present a conclusion in advance of the evidence on which it is based. This is, briefly, that the Ego is made up of the persisting elements, in the adult psyche, of the original nature of the child.

Certain aspects of the infant's psyche may be usefully examined. There are three factors that should receive mention. The first is, as Freud observed in his priceless phrase "His Majesty, the Baby," that the infant is born ruler of all he surveys. He comes from the nirvana of the womb, where he is usually the sole occupant, and he clings to that omnipotence with an innocence, yet determination, that baffles parent after parent. The second, stemming directly from the monarch within, is that the infant tolerates frustration poorly and lets the world know it readily. The third significant aspect of the child's original psyche is its tendency to do everything in a hurry. Observe youngsters on the beach: They run rather than walk. Observe them coming on a visit: The younger ones tear from the car while their elder siblings adopt a more leisurely pace. The three-year-olds, and more so the twos, cannot engage in play requiring long periods of concentration. Whatever they are doing must be done quickly. As the same children age, they gradually become able to stick to one activity for longer times.

Thus at the start of life the psyche (1) assumes its own omnipotence, (2) cannot accept frustrations, and (3) functions at a *tempo allegretto* with a good deal of *staccato* and *vivace* thrown in.

Now the question is, "If the infantile psyche persists into adult life, how will its presence be manifested?"

In general, when infantile traits continue into adulthood, the person is spoken of as immature, a label often applied with little comprehension of the reason for its accuracy. It is necessary to link these three traits from the original psyche with immaturity and, at the same time, show how they affect the adult psyche. If this is done, not only will the correctness of the appellation *immature* be apparent but, moreover, a feeling for the nature of the unconscious underpinnings of the Ego will have been created.

Recognizing Immaturity

Two steps can aid in recognizing the relationship between immaturity and a continuance of the infantile elements. The first is, by an act of imagination, to set these original traits into an adult unconscious. The validity of this procedure is founded upon modern knowledge of the nature of the forces operating in the unconscious of people of mature age. The second step is to estimate the effect that the prolongation of these infantile qualities will have upon the adult individual.

This attempt should not strain the imagination severely. Take, for instance, the third of the qualities common to the original psychic state, namely, the tendency to act hurriedly. If that tendency prevails in the unconscious, what must the result be? The individual will certainly do everything in a hurry. He will think fast, talk fast, and live fast, or he will spend an inordinate amount of time and energy holding his fast-driving proclivities in check.

Often the net result will be an oscillation between periods of speeding ahead followed by periods during which the direction of the force is reversed, the brakes (superego) being applied in equally vigorous fashion. The parallel of this in the behavior of the alcoholic will not be lost on those who have had experience with this class of patients.

Let us take the same trait of doing everything in a hurry and apply it to the word *immature*. Few will deny that jumping at conclusions, doing things as speedily as possible, give evidence of immaturity. It is youth that drives fast, thinks fast, feels fast, moves fast, acts hastily in most situations. There can be little question that one of the hallmarks of the immature is the proneness to be under inner pressure for accomplishment. Big plans, big schemes, big hopes abound, unfortunately not matched by an ability to produce. But the effect upon the adult of the persisting infantile quality to do everything in less than sufficient time can now be seen in a clearer light. The adult trait is surely a survival from the original psyche of the infant.

The two other surviving qualities of the infantile psyche similarly contribute to the picture of immaturity and also, indirectly, help to clarify the nature of the Ego with a capital *E*. The first of these, the feeling of omnipotence, when carried over into adult life, affects the individual in ways easily anticipated. Omnipotence is, of course, associated with royalty, if not divinity. The unconscious result of the persistence of this trait is that its bearer harbors a belief of his own special role and in his own exceptional rights. Such a person finds it well-nigh impossible to function happily on an ordinary level. Obsessed with divine afflatus, the thought of operating in the lowly and humble areas of life is most distressing to him. The very idea that such a place is all one is capable of occupying is in itself a blow to the Ego, which reacts with a sense of inferiority at its failure to fill a more distinguished position. Moreover, any success becomes merely Ego fodder, boosting the individual's rating of himself to increasingly unrealistic proportions as the king side eagerly drinks in this evidence of special worth.

The ability to administer the affairs of state, both large and small, is taken for granted. The belief that he is a natural executive placed in the wrong job merely confirms his conviction that, at best, he is the victim of lack of appreciation, and at worst, of sabotage by jealous people who set up roadblocks to his progress. The world is inhabited by selfish people, intent only on their own advancement.

The genesis of all this is beyond his perception. To tell him that his reactions spring from the demands of an inner unsatisfied king is to invite incredulity and disbelief, so far from the conscious mind are any such thoughts or feelings. People who openly continue to cling to their claims of divine prerogative usually end up in a world especially constructed for their care. In others, the omnipotence pressures are rather better buried. The individual may admit that, in many ways, he acts like a spoiled brat, but he is scarcely conscious of the extent of the tendency, nor how deeply rooted it may be. He, like most people, resolutely avoids a careful look because the recognition of any such inner attitudes is highly disturbing. The unconscious credence in one's special prerogatives savors too much of straight selfishness to be anything but unpleasant to contemplate.

And so, for the most part, people remain happily ignorant of the unconscious drives that push them around. They may wonder why they tend to boil inside and wish

they could free themselves from a constant sense of uneasiness and unsettlement. They may recognize that they
seem jittery and easily excited and long for the time
when they can meet life more calmly and maturely; they
may hate their tendency to become rattled. But their insight into the origin of all this is next to nothing, if not a
complete blank. The king lies deep below the surface, far
out of sight.

Inability to Accept Frustration

The last trait carried over from infancy is the inability to
accept frustration. In an obvious sense, this inability is another aspect of the king within, since one of the prerogatives of royalty is to proceed without interruption. For
the king to wait is an affront to the royal rank, a slap at his
majesty. The ramifications of this inability to endure
frustration are so widespread, and the significance of
much that occurs in the behavior of the alcoholic is so
far-reaching, that it seems advisable to discuss this trait
under a separate heading.

As already indicated, on the surface the inability of the
king to accept frustration is absolutely logical. The wish
of the king is the law of the land, and especially in the
land of infancy. Any frustration is clearly a direct threat
to the status of his majesty, whose whole being is chal-
lenged by the untoward interruption.

Even more significant is another aspect of this inner
imperiousness. Behind it lies the assumption that the individual should not be stopped. Again, this is logical if
one considers how an absolute monarch operates. He
simply does not expect to be stopped; as he wills, so will
he do. This trait, persisting in the unconscious, furnishes
a constant pressure driving the individual forward. It says,
in essence, "I am unstoppable!"

The unconscious, which cannot be stopped, views life entirely from the angle of whether or not a stopping is likely, imminent, or not at all in the picture. When a stopping is likely, there is worry and perhaps depression. When it seems imminent, there is anxiety bordering on panic, and when the threat is removed, there is relief and gaiety. Health is equated with a feeling of buoyancy and smooth sailing ahead, a sense of "I feel wonderful!" Sickness, contrariwise, means lacking vim, vigor, and vitality, and is burdened with a sense of "I'm not getting anywhere." The need to "get somewhere," to "be on the go," and the consequent suffering from eternal restlessness, is still another direct effect of an inner inability to be stopped or, expressed otherwise, to accept the fact that one is limited. The king not only cannot accept the normal frustrations of life but, because of his inordinate driving ahead, is constantly creating unnecessary roadblocks by virtue of his own insistence on barging ahead, thus causing added trouble for himself.

Of course, on some occasions, the king gets stopped, and stopped totally. Illness, arrest, sometimes the rules and regulations of life, will halt him. Then he marks time, complies if need be, waiting for the return of freedom, which he celebrates in the time-honored fashion if he is an alcoholic: He gets drunk, initiating a phase when there is no stopping him.

The immaturity of such a person is readily evident. He is impatient of delay, can never let matters evolve; he must have a blueprint to follow outlining clearly a path through the jungle of life. The wisdom of the ages is merely shackling tradition that should make way for the freshness, the insouciance of youth. The value of staying where one is, and working out one's destiny in the here and now, is not suspected. The twenty-four-hour principle would be confining for one whose inner life brooks no confinement. The unstoppable person seeks life, fun, adventure, excitement, and discovers he is on a perpetual whirligig that carries him continuously ahead—but, of course, in a circle. The unstoppable person has no time for growth. He must always, inwardly, feel immature.

This, then, is how the carryover of infantile traits affects the adult so encumbered. He is possessed by an inner king who not only must do things in a hurry but has no capacity for taking frustration in stride. He seeks a life that will not stop him and finds himself in a ceaseless rat race.

All this is part and parcel of the big Ego. The individual has no choice. He cannot select one characteristic and hang on to that, shedding other more obviously undesirable traits. It is all or nothing. For example, the driving person usually has plenty of energy, sparkle, vivacity. He stands out as a most attractive human being. Clinging to that quality, however, merely ensures the continuance of excessive drive and Ego, with all the pains attendant upon a life based on those qualities. The sacrifice of the Ego elements must be total, or they will soon regain their ascendancy.

Learning to Live

Those who view the prospect of life without abundant drive as inutterably dull and boring should examine the life of members of Alcoholics Anonymous who have truly adopted the AA program. They will see people who have been stopped—and who, therefore, do not have to go anywhere—but people who are learning, for the first time in their lives, to live. They are neither dull nor wishy-washy. Quite the contrary, they are alive and interested in the realities about them. They see things in the large, are tolerant, open-minded, not close-minded, bulling ahead. They are receptive to the wonders in the world about them, including the presence of a Deity who makes all this possible. They are the ones who are really living. The attainment of such a way of life is no mean accomplishment.

Preliminary to this discussion, the conclusion was offered that the Ego was a residual of the initial feeling life of the infant. It should be evident that the immaturity characteristically found in the makeup of the alcoholic is a persistence of the original state of the child. In connection with the description of the manifestations that denote a large and active Ego, it should be recalled that the presence in the unconscious of such Ego forces may be quite out of reach of conscious observation. Only through the acting and feeling of the individual can their existence be suspected.

Now the answer to the first question raised herein, namely, what part of the alcoholic must surrender, is obvious: It is the Ego element.

Life without Ego is no new conception. Two thousand years ago, Christ preached the necessity of losing one's life in order to find it again. He did not say Ego, but that was what he had in mind. The analysts of our time recognize the same truth; they talk also about ego reduction. Freud saw therapy as a running battle between the original narcissism of the infant (his term for Ego) and the therapist, whose task it was to reduce that original state to more manageable proportions. Since Freud could not conceive of life without some measure of Ego, he never resolved the riddle of how contentment is achieved; for him, man to the end was doomed to strife and unhappiness, his dearest desires sure to be frustrated by an unfriendly world.

In his studies on the addictions, Radó more explicitly asserts that the Ego must be reduced. He first portrays the Ego as follows: "Once it was a baby, radiant with self-esteem, full of belief in the omnipotence of its wishes, of its thoughts, gestures and words." Then, on the process of Ego-reduction: "But the child's megalomania melted away under the inexorable pressure of experience. Its sense of its own sovereignty had to make room for a more modest self-evaluation. This process, first described by Freud, may be designated the reduction in size of the original ego; it is a painful procedure and one that is possibly never completely carried out."[5]

No Compromise with Ego

Like Freud, Radó thinks only in terms of reduction; the need for the complete elimination of Ego is a stand that they cannot bring themselves to assume. Hence they unwittingly advocate the retention of some infantile traits, with no clear awareness that trading with the devil, the Ego, no matter how carefully safeguarded, merely keeps him alive and likely at any occasion to erupt full force into action. There can be no successful compromise with Ego, a fact not sufficiently appreciated by many, if not most, therapists.

Thus the dilemma encountered in ego reduction would be best resolved by recognizing that the old Ego must go, and a new one take its place. Then no issue would arise about how much of the earliest elements may be retained. The answer, theoretically, is none. Actually the total banishment of the initial state is difficult to achieve. Man can only grow in the direction of its complete elimination. Its final expulsion is a goal that can only be hoped for.

The second question raised here is, "How does the

surrender reaction change the inner psychic picture?" This question is based on a presupposition, namely, that surrender is an emotional step in which the Ego, at least for the time being, acknowledges that it is no longer supreme. This acknowledgment is valueless if limited to consciousness; it must be accompanied by similar feelings in the unconscious. For the alcoholic, surrender is marked by the admission of being powerless over alcohol. His sobriety has that quality of peace and tranquillity that makes for a lasting quiet within only if the surrender is effective in the unconscious and permanent as well.

The effects of surrender upon the psyche are extremely logical: The traits listed as characteristic of the Ego influence are canceled out. The opposite of king is the commoner. Appropriately, Alcoholics Anonymous stresses humility. The opposite of impatience is the ability to take things in stride, to make an inner reality of the slogan "Easy does it." The opposite of drive is staying in one position, where one can be open-minded, receptive, and responsive.

This picture of the non-Ego type of person might be amplified in many directions but to do so would serve no immediate purpose. To have discussed the effect of the Ego upon behavior, and to have pointed out what may happen when the Ego is at least temporarily knocked out of action, is sufficient to make the point of this communication: It is the Ego that is the archenemy of sobriety, and it is the Ego that must be disposed of if the individual is to attain a new way of life.

Up to this point, no clinical material has been submitted to confirm the ideas presented. Their validity will be apparent to many therapists. One brief citation from clinical experience will be offered, however, in the hope that it may serve as a concrete illustration of these ideas.

The patient, a man in his late thirties, had a long history of alcoholism, with seven years of futile attempts to recover through Alcoholics Anonymous, interspersed with countless admissions to "drying out" places. Then, for reasons not completely clear, he decided to take a drastic step. He determined to enter a sanatorium and place himself in the hands of a psychiatrist, a hitherto unheard-of venture. He telephoned to arrange for a limited stay at a sanatorium where he could have regular interviews with me.

From the outset, he was undeniably in earnest, although it was only after the first interview that he really let go and could talk freely about himself and the things that were going on inside him. After the usual preliminaries, the first interview started with a discussion of feelings and how they operate. The patient was questioned about the word *Ego* as used at AA meetings. He confessed his ignorance of its true meaning and listened with interest to brief remarks on how it works. Before long, he was locating in himself some of the Ego forces that hitherto he had been vigorously denying because they savored too much of vanity and selfishness.

With that recognition, the patient made a revealing remark. He said, in all sincerity, "My goodness, I never knew that. You don't do your thinking up here [pointing to his head], you think down here where you feel" [placing his hands on his stomach]. He was learning that his feelings had a "mind" of their own and that unless he heeded what they were saying, he could easily get into trouble. He was facing the actuality of his Ego as a feeling element in his life, a step he was able to take because he was no longer going at full steam ahead. His decision to place himself under care, a surrender of a sort, had quieted him and made him receptive, able to observe what was going on in himself. It was the beginning of a real inventory.

The next insight he uncovered was even more startling. He had been requested routinely to report any dreams he would have. Much to his surprise, they appeared regularly during the period of contact. In his fifth dream, the patient found himself locked up in an institution because of his drinking. The interpretation offered, based upon relevant materials, was that the patient equated any kind of stopping with being locked up; that his real difficulty lay in the fact that he could not tolerate being stopped, and abstaining was merely another stopping he could not take. The patient's reaction to the interpretation was most significant. He remained silent for some little time; then he began to talk, saying, "I tell you, Doc, it was like this. I'd get drunk, maybe stay on it two or three days, then I'd go into one of those drying out places where I'd stay five or six days and I'd be all over wanting a drink. Then I'd come out and stay sober, maybe a week, maybe a month, but pretty soon the thought would come into my mind, I want to drink! Maybe I'd go into a tavern and maybe not, but sooner or later I'd go and I'd order a drink, but I wouldn't drink it right off. I'd put it on the bar and I'd look at it and I'd think and then I'd look and think: King for a day!" The connection between Ego and his own conduct had become explicit, as well as the relationship between not being stopped and Ego. He saw clearly that when he took that drink, he was the boss once more. Any previous reduction of Ego had been only temporary.

In treatment, the problem is to make that reduction permanent. Therapy is centered on the ways and means, first, of bringing the Ego to earth, and second, keeping it there. The discussion of this methodology would be out of place here, but it is relevant to emphasize one point, namely, the astonishing capacity of the Ego to pass out of the picture and then reenter it, blithe and intact. A patient's dream neatly depicted this quality. This patient dreamt that he was on the twelfth-floor balcony of a New York hotel. He threw a rubber ball to the pavement below and saw it rebound to the level of the balcony. Much to his amazement, the ball again dropped and again rebounded to the same height. This continued for an indefinite period and, as he was watching, a clock in a neighboring church spire struck nine. Like the cat with nine lives, the Ego has a marvelous capacity to scramble back to safety—a little ruffled, perhaps, but soon operating with all its former aplomb, convinced once more that now it, the Ego, can master all events and push on ahead.

The capacity of the Ego to bypass experience is astounding and would be humorous were it not so tragic in its consequences. Cutting the individual down to size and making the results last is a task never completely accomplished. The possibility of a return of his Ego must be faced by every alcoholic. If it does return, he may refrain from drinking, but he will surely go on a "dry drunk," with all the old feelings and attitudes once more asserting themselves and making sobriety a shambles of discontent and restlessness. Not until the ego is decisively retired can peace and quiet again prevail. As one sees this struggle in process, the need for the helping hand of a Deity becomes clearer. Mere man alone all too often seems powerless to stay the force of his Ego. He needs assistance and needs it urgently.

Summary

In the process of surrender that the alcoholic necessarily undergoes before his alcoholism can be arrested, the part of the personality that must surrender is the inflated Ego. This aspect of personality was identified as immature traits carried over from infancy into adulthood, specifically, a feeling of omnipotence, inability to tolerate frustration, and excessive drive, exhibited in the need to do all things precipitously. The manner in which surrender affects the Ego was discussed and illustrated briefly from clinical experience. The object of therapy is to permanently replace the old Ego and its activity.

Alcoholics Anonymous:
An Experiment of Nature[1]

To Adolf Meyer every patient, in fact every person, was as an experiment of nature—a favorite phrase of his—the product of life forces within and without. He decried armchair speculation, stressing that the pertinent facts must be gathered before one could begin to see the reasons for an individual's behavior. He taught his students to view each individual as a newly evolved unit from which one could learn by keeping his eyes and ears open and tuning in on what nature had produced. He urged them to treat nature with respect and to avoid preconceptions whenever a natural phenomenon presented itself for study.

Alcoholics Anonymous seems to be a phenomenon whose emergence must be taken as a fact of nature. According to Meyer's conception, AA should be treated as material for observation and study. To disregard AA because its practice does not follow accepted scientific procedure would be a shortsighted waste of clinical material.

Observation of individuals who have joined AA in fact reveals a striking clinical phenomenon that will be described in the first section herein. A second section will analyze four concepts that help produce this phenomenon. A third will attempt to summarize the interrelations of the four concepts and the phenomenon under discussion and deal with the relevance of these findings for the treatment of alcoholics.

Clinical Data

The first of my patients to join AA had been having a difficult time under my type of therapy until, after a particularly trying period, I gave her a copy of the book *Alcoholics Anonymous.* She read it, went to a meeting, and soon was an active member of the group. The change in her has been described as follows:

> After Alcoholics Anonymous began to take hold, changes in her personality became apparent. Her aggression subsided materially, her feeling of being at odds with the world disappeared, and with it vanished her tendency to suspect the motives and attitudes of others. A sense of peace and calm ensued with real lessening of inner tension; and the lines of her face softened, becoming gentler and more kindly. That hard inner core was being altered, altered sufficiently to bring about her sobriety for a period of five years.[2]

This is the change I have labeled *conversion.* It involved a deep shift in the patient's emotional tone, not consciously willed but arising from changes in the unconscious psychodynamics, which caused the disappearance of one set of feelings and the emergence of another and very different set. In the course of her experience in AA she had been converted, or transformed, from a negative state of mind to a positive one. The change had many of the earmarks of a religious conversion. The sweeping and rapid revision of the state of mind, proceeding without conscious direction, seemed best designated by the term *conversion.*

This change in the inner life was surprising at first. In time, it became evident not only that other AA's went though the same kind of transformation or conversion but that unless they did, and retained it, their chances of remaining sober were minimal. Quite obviously some discrete pattern of response was being touched off. Here a phenomenon, natural in the psychic life, could be observed and studied.

A second case, more dramatic and colorful than the first, will further illustrate the same kind of change. This patient, a woman in her middle thirties, had become an alcoholic before she was twenty; her marriage, home, and family were nearly wrecked. After many fruitless attempts had been made to get her to go to AA or to see a psychiatrist or to enter a sanatorium, she made a desperate, last-gasp effort to control her drinking. Failing utterly, and in the depths of despair, she called a friend who was in AA. The friend, wise in the ways of the alcoholic, came running; but in the intervening twenty minutes the patient had taken enough liquor to make her again stubbornly refuse to seek aid. However, the friend persisted and eventually, out of her own experience with liquor, she struck a note to which the patient responded by saying, "Yes, I'll go to the sanatorium."

With that "Yes, I'll go," a change began to take place within the patient. She felt freer, lighter, less harassed, and no longer full of fright. From then on she seemed a different person.

True to her promise, two days later she entered the sanatorium where I was a staff member. She was still manifestly in the glow of her new state of mind. I asked her to write out a list of words describing how she felt before and after agreeing to come to the sanatorium. Two days later she presented the following lists, with a spontaneous note alongside:

I Felt	I Feel	
unstable	at peace	I have learned
tense	safe	the meaning of
nervous	composed	humility and
afraid	relaxed	meditation.
guilty	contented	
ashamed	thankful	
pushed	cleansed	
incapable	sane	
uncertain	receptive	
unworthy	prayerful	
dismayed		

No one can study these lists and the added comment without realizing that something real and quite wonderful had happened in that woman. Moreover, she found herself freed from the pressure to drink, so that in the forty-eight hours before admission she had drunk nothing alcoholic, and two days later, when she set down the list of words, she was still free from any desire for a drink.

Again the word *conversion* seems to suit this woman's experience. The change was more rapid and intense than in the first example but the two experiences are essentially similar. They and many like them form a pattern that regularly appears if and when AA takes hold. Here in a ready-made package was a solution to the problem of alcoholism for these patients. The question was, "What did that package contain?"

Exploring the Phenomenon

The contents of that package will not be exhausted in the following exposition and can only be outlined here.

Of the four concepts or insights mentioned above, two were gleaned from talks with AA members. They are, first, that the alcoholic must "hit bottom" before he can be helped; and second, that he must develop and maintain humility. Neither of these ideas can have the same impact now that they did when they first became evident over twenty years ago. They were so alien to all prior clinical concepts that at first their significance almost escaped recognition. They have since led to two collateral concepts, however, and the four together have provided some insights at least about the conversion experience.

The two concepts derived from AA were *hitting bottom* and *humility*.

Hitting Bottom

Hitting bottom was fairly easy to incorporate. It meant that a crisis had developed in the life of the individual and that he felt he could not continue on the path he had been pursuing.

Alcoholism is a progressive disease, and the victim in the course of time senses this fact and begins to worry about the inroads his drinking is making upon his life. He is doing a poorer job, acting worse as a husband and parent, and enjoying his drinking less and less. At last a time comes when he hits what might be called an emotional bottom. The pattern of his life is changing and for the worse, his attempts at control, often concealed even from himself, have regularly failed, and the prospect ahead is frightening. He begins to despair, to see nothing but hopelessness ahead with pain and misery his lot for the rest of his life. He is shaken, desperate, sunk in depression. He has hit a low, he has hit bottom. At that point, he wants help.

The importance of the need to hit bottom as a prelude to recovery is now rather generally accepted. Back in 1939 the idea of letting the individual suffer until he cried for help had very little sanction in psychiatric circles. The psychiatrist was a source of love and support even though that support carried the patient upright to his grave. For a psychiatrist to say "He has to hit bottom" was new and horrifying.

It was not long before the soundness of the AA policy was obvious to all. It was the first clue as to how the individual could be stimulated to seek assistance. The need to let the alcoholic suffer seemed to have its logic and has established itself clinically. There is talk of high bottoms, low bottoms, and medium ones too. All these terms refer to an emotional state of hopelessness and an inner conviction that one cannot continue as one has been going. They all call for a change and they prepare the individual for it. The capacity of some individuals to hit bottom must also be accepted as a clinical fact. Hitting bottom is an essential element in the experiment of nature that is AA.

Humility

The need to gain and maintain humility was the second concept derived from AA. The wisdom of letting the individual suffer and hit bottom was easily apparent, but it was difficult to understand why he had to be left prone. Enlightenment came from an AA friend, one of the co-founders of that fellowship.

He had given an inspiring and moving talk and when, unexpectedly, I was invited to comment, I found myself speaking my appreciation with unwonted eloquence. After the meeting, as I started to say good-bye to him, he responded with a wave of the hand and the announcement that he was going out to get drunk.

It was not possible then to ask questions, because several patients had to be returned immediately to the sanatorium. The next time we met he made the challenging remark, "You've got a lot to learn about us drunks." And then he explained his strange response at the meeting: "Don't you know we drunks can't stand praise?"

Hitting bottom was only half the job for the alcoholic. The real task was to stay there. Praise could go to his head, cause it to swell, and make him feel once more that he could handle liquor. Humility could prevent that rebound.

The two concepts thus learned from AA were incorporated into a technique of treating the alcoholic: He may be helped to hit bottom, and then helped to avoid a return of the state of mind that had produced trouble previously. As a consequence of these policies, two clinical facts came into view. The first has been termed surrender; the second is the need for ego reduction.

Surrender

A patient first named it surrender. She had been under the new brand of therapy and had had a minor conversion experience, culminating in a positive state with sufficient religious overtones to send her to church for the first time in years. One Monday morning she entered the office with eyes sparkling. She declared that she knew what had happened to her, she had heard it in a hymn— she had "surrendered." With that, a new word entered my psychiatric vocabulary, although the fact was not recognized immediately.

The word was next heard from another patient, the same who had experienced the rapid conversion and had written the previously cited lists of words describing her before-and-after state. On one occasion, when I asked what had happened to her, she promptly replied, "I surrendered." It was startling to hear the same word a second time. To further questioning she replied, "Around here, they call it acceptance, but that's not so good; it still leaves a piece of *you.*" She knew that acceptance was only partial surrender and that real surrender freed the individual from all traces of the self that had been fighting the giving up of alcohol. The last vestige of that self had to be removed. Otherwise it would soon be sneaking in again and causing trouble.

This second encounter with the word fixed attention upon the concept of surrender. It is now clear that hitting bottom can produce a surrender and that without surrender an individual can hit bottom a thousand times without anything significant taking place.

The word *surrender* is in good favor in AA circles. Its members recognize it as descriptive and frequently use it in their talks when they tell of joining AA. One speaker began with the statement, "I surrendered to alcohol four years ago and haven't had a drop since." Others refer to the moment when they gave up the battle against liquor and call that a surrender. They are not being technical, they are using a word that has deep meaning for them because it describes what occurred when the AA process could take over.

The notion of surrender is no longer so widely rejected as it was formerly. The existentialists, when they advocate being oneself, advise one to let go and be. They view surrender as a letting go of control and presume that such dropping of the reins will permit greater spontaneity and naturalness and a greater sense of being a person. They occasionally use the word *surrender* and apparently are well aware that every individual needs to forego his place as pilot and boss and accept the lesser role of just being human. The note of humbleness is again being heard.

To "let go," to give up one's rigidities, to relax, to be oneself, is easier suggested than done. Moreover, the concept of letting go is confusing. It is one thing to let go and do as you please; it is quite a different matter to let go in surrender and do as the other person pleases. The first letting go is abandon and involves a way of life that few can follow. Few desire to remove themselves from human society as they would if governed by unrestrained instincts. Such isolation is unbearable.

To let go in surrender is a totally different step. Despair is its source; the feeling "I cannot go on" and "I am licked." All this is part of the crisis experience, with its overload of hopelessness. It is pounded home in AA by the first of its Twelve Steps which reads: "We admitted we were powerless over alcohol—that our lives had become unmanageable." The emphasis is on defeat, on acknowledging failure, that the situation is desperate, that the end is in sight.

Under such circumstances when an individual gives up he is not throwing off restraints, he is surrendering to them. He is saying in essence, perhaps for the first time in his life, "I can't go on as I please. You win, I lose." In AA language he has accepted a Power greater than himself. He has quit competing for his place in the ranks of the high and mighty. AA members would say that his ego has been reduced. And they are right. A surrender experience reduces the individual's ego, a development from which, as a person, he profits enormously. The problem of ego reduction is one that can be discussed only tentatively and not without considerable misgivings.

Ego Reduction

Apparently it is the ego that shuns surrender, and when a surrender has occurred, it means that the ego has lost its grip. But the matter cannot be understood without first settling the question, "What ego are we talking about?" It is essential to clarify a real difficulty in terminology.

The word *ego* has both a technical usage and a popular one. The analytically oriented tend to discard the popular concept of ego as unscientific and not worthy of serious consideration. Nevertheless, the popular usage of the word has a profound validity, and any ignoring of the popular definition of ego can be a cause of confusion.

In psychiatric circles, the meaning attached to *ego* is that which rests on the division of the psyche into three major functions, the id, the superego, and the ego. Freud approximately placed the feelings in the id, the conscience in the superego, and control in the ego. Freud's insight into the ego forces never achieved such development as his ideas on the id and the superego and their functions, and it is in this direction especially that his pupils and others have been extending their knowledge during recent decades.

They have investigated how the ego is formed, how it operates, and how it can be helped to serve its function most usefully. As a consequence of their studies, the word *ego* has come to represent a whole area of conscious and unconscious mentation; although this area is hard to define exactly, those working in the field have some common awareness of it and can discuss it with mutual understanding. For those who think in terms of Freud's divisions of the psyche, the word *ego,* in spite of its somewhat nebulous definition, is a helpful term designating a group of psychic activities and forces. For them, any other use of the word is disturbing and distracting.

Yet the word *ego* has its place in everyday language. The individual with the "big ego" is generally pictured as thinking well of himself, giving himself high priority, although he may be bending over backward to avoid making this impression. People are called egoists or are said to be egotistical.

The word used in this sense is completely meaningful. It has entered the language and has a rightful place in it because it expresses an idea clearly. The linkage between *ego* as a word and big *ego* as a concept seems likely to persist in living language. Within recent time it has appeared in articles about the disputes between labor and management and about the protocol between nations or in the Senate. It has been used editorially in *The New York Times*. There is no escape from recognizing the existence of two meanings of *ego*, nor from dealing with the two different concepts represented by them.

As Freud conceived it, the ego was an emergent that appeared as the id was modified. It is manifested by an individual developing a capacity to think, to reason, to exercise his will, and by his gaining a central focus around which these faculties become organized. When these faculties are working well, the ego is held to be healthy. The ego in this framework is the control mechanism. It should have the final say, although it does not always succeed in maintaining itself against the pressures of the id and the superego.

Freudian psychiatry held that this ego should be strong and capable of asserting its prerogatives and that a weak ego requires strengthening to give it the power to hold its own against the onslaughts of the other two elements in the psyche. But nowhere in this scheme is that big ego represented that people observe and that disappears after a surrender and conversion experience.

It seems possible now to state what this big ego represents, at least in the form of a hypothesis.

In his article on narcissism, speaking of what must

happen to the original psyche, Freud wrote: "The development of the ego consists in a departure from the primary narcissism and results in a vigorous attempt to defend it."[3] Radó in 1933, referring to the psyche at birth, said, "Once it was a baby, radiant with self-esteem, full of belief in the omnipotence of its wishes, of its thoughts, gestures and words."[4] He then proceeded to the subject of ego change:

> But the child's megalomania melted away under the inexorable pressure of experience. Its sense of its own sovereignty had to make room for a more modest self-evaluation. This process, first described by Freud, may be designated the reduction in the size of the original ego; it is a painful procedure and one that is possibly never completely carried out.

The big ego encountered in people in everyday life appears to be a manifestation of the original ego of the infant, a narcissistic remnant, a carryover of the infantile state. Freud would have called it an unmodified portion of the original psyche. If this narcissistic quality persists, it will serve as a source for a narcissistic type of ego, notably an egocentric one. In other words, the big ego is a popular designation for an ego filled with narcissistic components.

According to Freudian concepts, the modification of the infantile ego is an essential development. There is no reason to believe that this modification is ever total, so that roughly any ego can be divided into two aspects, namely that which has been modified and that which has not. Thus the person with the big ego is suffering from an ego in which the unmodified aspect is dominant, though it may be presumed that some modification has occurred.

Granting this division, the therapist's dual responsibility becomes clear. He must do what he can to reduce the power of the narcissistic components and at the same time help to increase the position and prestige of the components that have been modified. Ego reduction is limited to the narcissistic elements; if their influence can be sufficiently neutralized, the patient will no longer be dominated by these immature elements.

Weeding out immaturities and, at the same time, supporting the elements that manifest the modified ego is a tricky business. Unless the therapist is careful, he will hinder rather than help. For instance, the need for a strong and efficient ego, able to manage the id and the superego, is thought by most psychiatrists to be essential for a healthy psyche. The narcissistic elements within the ego, however, revel in being told to be strong. Thus if a patient learns of the need for ego strength but understands ego according to the popular conception with which he is familiar, he is less susceptible to ego reduction than he was to begin with.

When the distinction between technical usage and the popular one is laid before him, he may admit that he is strengthening only a part of his ego—and the wrong part, at that—but deep inside he cannot believe it. The immature side gains support and new reason for continuing to defend itself. It becomes more fixed and rigid than before. The patient must travel a considerable distance in therapy before it dawns on him that what he has mistaken for strength is a frozen rigidity that keeps him tense and precludes letting go and the chance to become himself.

Thus a therapist's failure to take into account what ego probably means to the patient can cause a serious distortion which hinders treatment rather than helping it. Every therapist must be constantly vigilant on this score.

On the other hand, making the proper distinction between the two types of ego response can increase understanding. The concept of ego reduction is a case in point.
People in general shy away from the notion—even in the
abstract—that someone's ego should be reduced. It is understandable, then, that strong resistance may be encountered when the patient is faced with the threat of his own
ego being reduced. If at this point the therapist can help
the patient make the distinction between the two aspects
of the ego and to understand that the ego in question is
the one derived from infantile sources, then ego reduction becomes an end tolerable and even desirable. In no
other way can the individual mature.

Similarly, the concept of surrender loses its odious con-
notations. When the patient is helped to recognize that it
is the same infantile ego that must surrender, his fear of
surrender as a sign of weakness can be supplanted by the
knowledge that surrender is a necessary step in the maturation process. Only through surrender can the modification occur. As long as the original ego condition stays
inviolate, its defenses intact, no change can take place.
Only as these defenses are shattered through the crisis
experience can the individual be opened up to change
and thus to be modified. The idea of keeping the infantile ego inviolate is obviously untenable. Surrender, when
it happens, is part and parcel of the process, of altering
that initial state and thus a needed element in growing
up. To shun a consideration of its significance is to repeat
the error about ego reduction and to ensure unwittingly
a perpetuation of the infantile attitudes.

The term *ego reduction,* then, must not be applied to
the ego that Freud conceived of when he divided the
psyche into three major areas; it refers to the process he
was anticipating when he said that "the development of

the ego [here used in his own sense] consists in a departure from the primary narcissism [i.e., *ego* in the popular sense, the infantile aspect of the Freudian ego] and results in a vigorous attempt to defend it."[5]

In 1933 Radó could be and was more explicit about this primary narcissism and what must happen to it. He wrote, "Once it [the original ego] was a being, radiant with self-esteem, full of belief in the omnipotence of its wishes, of its thoughts, gestures and words." (Freud had summed it up in the phrase, "His Majesty, the Baby.") After this description, Radó continues with the phrase, "But the child's megalomania"—a direct reference to the big head or big ego that the infant has at birth. And then, in the sequel, he specifically makes the ego the target and uses the word *reduction* to describe what must take place: "This process, first described by Freud, may be designated the reduction in the size of the original ego; it is a painful procedure and one that is possibly never completely carried out."[6]

And, incidentally, he had said that reduction could produce "a more modest self-evaluation," which certainly indicates that the individual becomes more humble. There is no doubt that he had a feel for what happens within the person as the narcissistic ego elements are reduced.

In passing, it may be of interest to note the choice of the words *departure* and *reduction*. Freud spotted the area of change and said it must be departed from. Radó, from the vantage of many years later, said the change must be a reduction, a clear statement about the direction of the departure. Radó even uses the word *size* when he speaks of the original ego, a word which appears in the phrase "cuts down to size," a well-known colloquialism that vividly suggests what happens to the big ego.

The experience of a patient who had a "slip" is clinically illuminating of the meaning of ego reduction. A slip, of course, is a short or long period of drinking by an alcoholic who has had a period of sobriety of some duration. It is seldom, if ever, willed and very often occurs without obvious external reason. A woman in her early forties had done well under a regimen of AA, disulfiram, and psychotherapy. She was pleased with her progress and was toying with the idea of terminating the psychotherapy since she was not sure she still needed it.

During the summer recess the patient stopped taking the disulfiram tablets and was slack about attending AA meetings. "I had done so well, I thought they weren't urgent any more," was her subsequent explanation. Then one day, for no apparent reason, she took a drink. This proved not disastrous because, after a couple of days of struggle, she was able through AA help to quit drinking and soon was dutifully taking disulfiram again.

However, she promptly made sure she was on my autumn schedule and, when she appeared for her first interview, was full of the story she had to tell. "You know," she said, "no one was more surprised than I was when I took that first drink. Everything had been fine and I had no worries at all. Then I decided to have a drink and I did. For the life of me, I can't tell you why, because I really didn't enjoy it."

She then went on, "Even as I was taking that drink, I was asking myself why I was doing this. I wondered what explanation Doctor Tiebout would have for this. Then I suddenly remembered a dream I had had the night before, and I wondered if it had any significance. Here it is. I wrote it down right away."

This is what she had written: "I was looking at a suit

of armor that was scattered all over the floor. I was trying to reassemble it and finally did."

The message of this dream is clear. Once she reassembled her nice, hard covering, her ego (in the popular sense) was again intact, and at that point she could take a drink and did. As the patient grasped the significance of her dream, her eyes twinkled and she said, "You know, the word *reassembled* is not a word I very often use. But as I was writing the dream down, I came to trying to say what happened to that armor, and the word *reassembled* came into my mind. I thought it rather odd but I wrote it down just as you have told me to. It makes a lot more sense to me now than it did when I put it down. I guess my unconscious knew what had happened all right although I certainly was not aware of it when I took that first drink."

The dream, of course, illustrates the opposite of ego reduction. The reduced ego, scattered, unintact, made sobriety possible. But the patient was unable to maintain that state. Just like the man who said he was going to get drunk after being praised, this patient could not stand the prosperity of sobriety. She was on her own and there was no doctor, no AA, no disulfiram as chemical fence, no daily reminder that would keep that ego down. And she did not have the capacity to keep it down by herself, a fact she had yet to learn. Once her ego got unreduced or "reassembled," she was headed for trouble, which came the very next day.

Her unconscious knew what it was doing when it injected the word *reassembled* into her thinking. It was stating, "The period of reduction is over and now I can reassert myself." A drink the next day was the outcome.

At one time, not long ago, the message of this dream might have been lost. With the role of the narcissistic aspect of the ego better understood, it is possible to pick up such messages. This dream was particularly striking because its antecedents could be readily identified, and its effect upon the unconscious was easily determined by the onset of drinking the next day.

Another patient had a different reaction to the issue of ego reduction. She had been in AA for many years and had come for help because she suffered from periods of tension bordering on panic. She had been under treatment for some time when she began to face more concretely the problems of ego reduction. Characteristically this process is often equated with the "fall of man from his high estate," i.e., loss of omnipotence. The patient ushered in this phase with a dream in which she reported: "My niece fell off a ladder." The patient had a strong identification with this niece, who was practically a daughter. It was quite evident who was falling.

The next dream found the patient visiting a dentist. There was also something about a funeral in the dream. The inner response to ego reduction was now being revealed. Teeth often stand for bite and, in turn, stand for strength, i.e., "bite your teeth into it." Anyone going to a dentist is receiving attention for his bite, that is, something is threatening it with impairment. At the same time, the patient has death in the offing, a direct reference to the belief that, if the ego falls, it is the equivalent of psychic death. Actually, of course, this is the part of the ego the individual must lose if he is to mature. The patient's reaction to falling is to fear death and to seek dental attention in the hope that her bite can be repaired.

The immediately following dream began with the statement "Drinking." The patient had her own method of recapturing her bite—by taking a drink. Fortunately, this proved only a dream act, although the patient reported general uneasiness extending over several days.

This case again illustrates how unconscious reactions may be deciphered if the therapist is alert to the theme of the fall and rise of the ego elements that stem from the original narcissism. These elements wage a constant battle. Their presence, actual or potential, is a factor always to be kept in awareness.

Discussion

This discussion of ego reduction has completed the presentation of the four insights that grew out of a study of the conversion process first witnessed in AA. To recapitulate, these are

1. the need to hit bottom
2. the need to be humble
3. the need to surrender
4. the need for the primary ego to be reduced

Bringing them all together but slightly transposing their order, we can say that a conversion occurs when the individual hits bottom, surrenders, and thereby has his ego reduced. His salvation lies in keeping that ego reduced, in staying humble.

These insights, gained from a long study of Alcoholics Anonymous and the process it initiates, appear to give meaning and order to the change that AA induces. Conversion is no longer an event "out of the blue" but a logical outgrowth of human responses: hitting bottom and surrender.

This does not imply complete comprehension of the mysteries of the conversion process. That still remains a marvel about which many questions have yet to be answered. But this understanding seems to touch on some

of the forces at work, forces that evidently are of profound importance to man. If this understanding only
scratches the surface of these psychological events, it
nevertheless seems to tell a great deal about how man
changes.

Two issues raised by the preceding discussion require
particular attention: First, the specific problem of how
the word *ego* should be handled in clinical practice; second, the general problem of the therapeutic situation,
especially in its earliest phase, with surrender and ego reduction in mind.

The problem of the word *ego* should be tackled early.
For instance, one aspect of the narcissistic ego is that it
must be the master, must feel that it is in control. Very
commonly a patient's first dreams will demonstrate this
point. Typically he will be driving a car, i.e., be in the
driver's seat, and then will get out, thereby showing that
in therapy he must forgo for a while running his life on
his own say-so.

When a dream of this type occurs, it is appropriate to
alert the patient to the feelings which are aroused when
one is driving a car: the sense of well-being, the headi-
ness that comes from being the "boss-man." He easily
grasps what is meant and is puzzled that the therapist
should raise any question about that side of his nature.
The matter may be allowed to rest there for a while. As
time goes on, the patient realizes that there are other less
desirable aspects of the same ego elements. They are
domineering and "pushy"; they withstand frustration
poorly; basically they cause him to be afraid of his own
shadow—or, more accurately, of his own drives that, he
soon learns, are rather imperious forces.

As this awareness grows, the individual commences to
detach himself from these elements and to discover that

he has another side that is a little quieter, a little less strenuous, a little more patient, and a little less in need of having all the answers and being in control. This may be referred to, for the patient's benefit, as the other self or just the self; sometimes as the more sensible side or the less driven part of one's nature. This self is the ego that appears as the original ego is modified, and this newly emerging ego should never be identified with the word *ego*. It is too confusing for patients. Instead, with them, the word *ego* should be confined to its more popular meaning. They catch on without trouble and in a relatively short time are thinking in terms of ego reactions and nonego ones. They go around spotting big fat egos in everyone and begin to see more clearly how ego of this type concerns themselves.

As therapy continues, if it is going well, the ego they first encountered in themselves slowly recedes and they become more and more identified with the other self, which is growing as a real element in their makeup. The time comes, ideally, when this new self supersedes the former and the individual is free from the harassments of the big ego he once had.

This description of the course of therapy is not new. The only step that may be different is the aim to get the patient as soon as possible to realize that his concept of ego is not one that can be maintained and that he must eventually find another self free from the unhealthy elements that he formerly took for granted, as he did being in the driver's seat.

When the original ego is identified early in therapy, the problem of nomenclature drops out. Patients fairly quickly recognize the two aspects of ego, although in practice they seldom call the new ego by that term. They will say, instead, "Some of me is coming through," and are more regardful of how they feel rather than how they ought to feel. The other self is slowly taking shape, and they are getting more and more in touch with it.

This is the self that needs support from the therapist. This support can be direct or indirect. In my experience, the most effective help the newly emerging self can receive is through an indirect approach. If the narcissistic side is reduced, the new self circumstantially has a chance to grow. To be sure, such growth may well be nurtured, but if the weeds of the original ego are removed the other self will develop with little or no urging.

Every therapy springs from some form of hitting bottom. The patient is brought to seek help either by the distress his symptoms create or by the exigencies of his life situation. In other words, every patient is motivated by a sense of crisis, which takes the form of not wanting the present situation to continue as it is. A change seems preferable, and the patient has not found a way of bringing it about by himself. He must seek help.

Now, the seeking of help is anathema to the strong narcissistic ego, which would go it alone, recoiling from help as a sign of weakness. As a consequence, the very seeking of help is an act of surrender, a giving up, and produces a characteristic chain of reactions. A graphic example is in the second list of words by the patient who consented to seek help: "at peace, relaxed, receptive," and so forth.

In that frame of mind, a prospective patient is a good candidate for therapy. He quickly takes on the therapist, develops a transference, and enters the honeymoon phase of treatment—mainly because he has quit fighting and has turned to another for help. He has given up, he is no longer going it alone, he has surrendered in fact, if not consciously.

The surrender, however, seldom is permanent. The motivation arising from the sense of crisis vanishes with the earliest improvement, the armor is reassembled, and the treatment is blocked by a phase of resistance. The conflict between the forces that seek help and those that fight it is now joined and the battle of treatment is on.

In other words, at the start of therapy the issue of surrender is immediately faced. The subsequent course of treatment can be predicted to a very considerable extent if the roles of hitting bottom, humility, surrender, and ego reduction are kept in mind as essential features in a therapeutic experience.

Summary

Based on observations of Alcoholics Anonymous as its program has effected change in many members, and from clinical experience with alcoholic patients, a hypothesis is formulated concerning the effective psychological events that make possible the maintenance of sobriety. Four elements are recognized as playing an essential role: hitting bottom, surrender, ego reduction, and maintenance of humility. The application of this conceptualization in individual psychotherapy is discussed and illustrated with case material.

Direct Treatment of a Symptom[1]

Therapists with alcoholics have a twofold task. They must treat the disease alcoholism, and they must treat the person afflicted with it. Psychiatrists have tended to bypass the disease and treat the individual, but again and again under this approach the patient has proved recalcitrant to all therapeutic endeavor. As a result, alcoholics have been considered very unlikely prospects for therapy of any sort.

The difficulty, of course, was in the main symptom of the disease: the fact that the patient would get drunk, which repeatedly nullified all attempts at assistance. As a consequence, work with the person who drank was stymied by the fact that he drank. In the face of this dilemma, therapists have thrown up their hands in dismay and have turned to greener pastures.

The mistake we made was our failure to recognize that the task was twofold. In rather doctrinaire fashion, we persisted in treating the alcoholism as a symptom that would be cured or arrested if its causes could be favorably altered. The drinking was something to be put up with as best as one could while more fundamental matters were being studied. The result of this procedure was that very few alcoholics were helped. The drinking continued and the symptom remained untouched.

In other medical treatment this concept of getting at causes is not considered sufficient. No one ignores a cancer, for instance, while searching for its origins. It is cut into or treated with X-ray or radium in the hope that the growth will either be removed or will stop advancing.

Once the cancer is detected, the question of etiology is academic.

Exactly the same thinking applies to the treatment of alcoholism. It is a symptom that becomes dangerous in itself. Until it has been effectively stopped, little of real help can be offered. Alcoholics Anonymous stresses the danger of the first drink, and Antabuse simply stops the ability to take it. Both attack the symptom and both have recorded a substantial measure of success.

The advent of these new tools not only has given us a means of treating the symptom directly, it has focused attention upon a factor whose importance was hitherto insufficiently appreciated. That factor is the significance of the *first drink* and what it represents to the psyche of the drinker.

Such focusing has two results. First, it directs thought toward the problem of stopping, that is, of not taking the first drink. Second, it leads to a new approach to the understanding of what must transpire in therapy if the alcoholic is to remain sober.

This paper will discuss both those points, namely, the direct treatment of a symptom and the individual's reaction to such a direct approach.

The Direct Treatment of a Symptom

The direct treatment of a symptom is and has been the subject of much controversy. A review of the past is necessary to set the controversy in perspective.

Roughly, we can divide the past into the time before Freud and the time after. Prior to his epoch-making revelations about the unconscious and its controlling influence over behavior, all treatment perforce was direct. If a person was acting in a disturbed manner, he was placed in an institution. If he broke the law, he was imprisoned.

A naughty child was spanked. Treatment was aimed at behavior and was essentially disciplinary, the big stick. For the most part, it was applied blindly, woodenly, as the only known means of combating the behaviors being encountered.

Then through Freud's work, conduct was recognized as an outgrowth of unconscious functioning, and, before long, the field of psychiatry embraced as one of its major tenets the principle that all behavior sprang from the unconscious, and that therapy, when necessary, had as its goal the determination and elimination of the pathology behind upsetting behavior. The validity of such a shift was indisputable. Since former blind methods could be replaced by much more precise measures, direct treatment of a symptom lost all caste. The day of scientific therapy had arrived.

Strangely, though, a new kind of woodenness then appeared. Anything prior to Freud was out, to be viewed dimly and with alarm.

I, too, was an early believer and expounder of the theory that all behavior was symptomatic. I, as much as anyone, searched energetically for unconscious forces to help alcoholics, and I, too, fell flat on my face. It just did not work.

Then, as related elsewhere,[2] Alcoholics Anonymous came along and I saw it succeed not only in arresting the drinking, but in helping a person to mature. All my pet assumptions were knocked into a cocked hat (and it took me many a year to realize the full import of what I had seen happen to my patient as she made the grade through Alcoholics Anonymous).

Unconcerned with causes and not bewitched by dogma, the AA program was designed to get the individual to stop drinking, and really nothing else. The aspects of personality inventory and of spiritual growth were useful in AA chiefly because they tended to ensure the individual's capacity for not taking the first drink. They had nothing to do with causation. The whole program was direct treatment of a symptom.

When this dawned, most of my previous thinking on getting at causes had to be shelved, placed to one side, so that this new fact could be studied open-mindedly.

Antabuse came along to confirm the soundness of tackling the symptom, and the need to find an explanation for that heretical fact became more imperative. Finally, the significance of the first drink became apparent, and then the corollary fact that the individual must stop taking even "one."

With the recognition that that was the goal of both methods, pre-Freud direct management of symptoms took on a different significance. This, too, was to be seen as an effort to change the individual's behavior either by putting him in an institution for the mentally ill, or by jailing him, or by inflicting punishment. To be sure, these techniques might be applied without much precision and perhaps too often, but they nevertheless effectively stopped the symptoms, and perhaps that, in and of itself, was not only useful but necessary. Certainly, insofar as helping the alcoholic was concerned, the direct method worked. In my eyes, such treatment had been reestablished as a sound clinical procedure and a valid tool. Hopefully, it could be applied with more skill and finesse now that the Freudian insights were available, but to dismiss it totally would be inexcusable rigidity and evidence of very unscientific dogmatism.

The Individual's Reaction

With the acceptance of the validity of the direct approach, the treatment of the alcoholic individual takes on a new dimension. Instead of determining causes, the therapeutic aim is directed toward helping the patient to utilize available techniques, AA, Antabuse, and/or psychiatry, to aid in his battle to stop drinking. The therapist, so to speak, has his prescription. His job is to sell it to the patient.

At this point, we run into a fundamental issue. Most patients take their doctor's prescription. Very few alcoholics respond that simply. As a result, the doctor has the task of inducing the patient to take the medicine offered, and it is here that we must consider the nature of the alcoholic, the individual who balks at taking the remedy suggested. This brings us to our second point, namely, the nature of the individual who so stubbornly refuses to stop drinking.

More accurately, the topic of this section is the nature of the individual's reaction to direct treatment. The physician for the alcoholic, regardless of his personal inclinations or his theoretical convictions about the function of the therapist, is placed in the role of someone who is trying to stop the patient's drinking. And although the alcoholic may desperately want help consciously, this does not necessarily overcome his unconscious resistance to such authoritative handling. The therapist inevitably acts as a depriving person.

To try to avoid that role is silly, misleading, and a very poor example. Silly because it denies the obvious, and misleading because it is attempting to sugarcoat an unpalatable truth. A poor example, because the therapist is denying reality—behavior at which the patient is already expert. Fundamental respect can never be established on such a false basis.

As a consequence, the therapist must not fight the patient's identification of him as a depriving figure. There is no loophole from that position. The only hope is to help the patient learn to accept deprivation and therefore reach a state in which, as a mature person, he will realize that all his wants and demands cannot be satisfied and that there are some things he cannot have.

The therapist must not sidestep his depriving role; instead he must freely acknowledge it and let therapy begin right there. To do so clears the atmosphere and paves the way for establishing a sound working relationship.

The following clinical material shows not only these new tactics that must be adopted but also the patient's reaction to them. The patient is a man in his middle thirties who, after six years of stumbling success with AA, decided to try psychiatry because, to quote him, "I'm almost as bad as when I started with AA. I've got to do something." It was clear that he was strongly motivated, and consequently he was accepted for therapy. The patient was told that his immediate problem was drinking and that it could ruin his chances of profiting from assistance. There would be no insistence on total sobriety, but there would be the following stipulation: If in my opinion his drinking was interfering with therapy, I could require him to take Antabuse, which would ensure sobriety over a period long enough to settle whether or not he could profit from treatment, so that later on he might be able to get along without the medication.

The patient promptly accepted this proviso, saying it made complete sense to him. On the surface he seemed completely receptive. He remarked in confirmation, "I know when I'm drinking it would be a waste of your time to try to help me; I just wouldn't get a thing." No trace of protest could be observed and I am sure none was felt. In fact the patient seemed to welcome a forthright statement of what lay before him. He at least knew where he stood.

Also during the first interview the patient was asked to record his dreams. At the next session, he reported the following:

1. irritated and teased pet bird
2. vaguely remembered X.Y., thought he was drinking with him
3. accidentally pulled all the tail feathers out of pet bird

The first dream he then expanded, adding, "The pet bird was mine and it was caged and visibly annoyed." Little imagination is required to read the unconscious thoughts at this point. Birds stand for freedom, i.e., "free as a bird." A caged bird is not free and, therefore, is "irritated" and "visibly annoyed," feelings that every freedom-loving person would show if caged. And no one would deny that a caged bird was a stopped one. The first dream pinpoints the fact that therapy was designed to stop drinking.

The next dream finds the patient drinking with a boon companion, a person he was prone to turn to after sobriety had begun to pall. In this dream, quite literally, the bird becomes the patient, escaped from the cage, and the cage that has been escaped from is the knowledge about the danger of the first drink.

The report of the third dream also received interesting amplification. The patient volunteered that the bird flew by him and that, as it did, he grabbed at it and "pulled every last tail feather off, and all that was left was a bare little butt end." Again the message of the dream is clear. The free bird, again in the picture, presents its butt end to the world, an unequivocal gesture of defiance.

The story that these dreams have to tell seems unambiguous. The patient is coming for help about his alcoholism, which he knows can be treated only by his not taking the first drink. The symbol of the caged and annoyed bird is a brilliant condensation of three aspects of his own self as it reacts to his new situation. First, the bird is a symbol of freedom; second, it represents the sense of restriction which is the cage; and third, it shows the "visible annoyance" and "frustration" that the bird feels as it is confronted by the fact that it is not at liberty. In the second dream the patient is no longer stopped. The third dream reveals this clearly as a defiant response to the therapy.

No doubt other interpretations with which I would have no dispute may be offered for these dreams. The point is, however, that the theme of stopping is also unmistakably present in the patient's unconscious, which shows a completely understandable reaction to the idea of being stopped and frustrated.

Despite the note of defiance on which they end, these dreams actually started therapy off on a good, sound basis. First and foremost, the patient learned that he had unconscious attitudes. Although he protested vigorously that he had no feeling of defiance toward either the doctor or the treatment, he knew that on many occasions he had shown and felt just such inner attitudes. He could now appreciate that defiance was in his system even contrary to his desires and in spite of his failure to be aware of it. From now on, he would have to recognize the presence of an inner-feeling life that psychiatry might help him reach and learn to handle better. Any lurking misgivings regarding psychiatry were to some extent lessened.

In addition, the patient had to face his inner demand to be free and that inside he balked at any curbing. Recognition of this fact was comforting, for it gave him a belief that further insights might be forthcoming and that the possibility of help might exist.

Still a third advantage to his start sprang from the discussion of defiance and the insistence upon freedom.

The patient's immediate reaction was to scold himself for acting that way and to feel guilty that he had allowed such attitudes to persist. When he could realize that these forces were deep-seated and real, he could drop his punitive reactions of guilt and focus upon the more important issue of how he could rid himself of his tendency to defy and his desire to cherish his freedom at the expense of his sanity. The burden of guilt could be lifted and with it the tensions that contributed so much to his drinking. Therapy was obviously under way.

As this example shows, the patient's negative responses to the direct approach need not be feared, because they can be used to suggest to the patient the idea that their very presence, while easy to comprehend, is an indication of where his trouble lies.

Let me summarize briefly the points made so far. First, the treatment of the alcoholic must initially focus on his drinking. To say this is not to ignore the person or his body. They must always receive attention regardless of the ailment. However, the primary emphasis on the control of the drinking is essential if treatment is to succeed. Second, the patient's reactions to direct treatment not only do not undermine the therapeutic relationship, but may actually enhance it. As those reactions are discovered and faced, a solid foundation for a good therapeutic experience is created. To act otherwise can only result in confusion.

Before closing, a few comments are in order.

First, the importance of timing cannot be overemphasized. The patient who reacted well to an active technique was ripe for the plucking. He wanted to quit and had been trying to for several years. He was a perfect candidate for the direct approach.

Actually he was at the end of a very long trail. It began

with his drinking blithely and unconcernedly. It was nearing its conclusion hopefully with his earnest desire not to take the first drink. Space limitations prevent my identifying and discussing all the various sections of that trail. Suffice it to say that he could now seek help with no conscious reservations.

Actually, such direct methods can be applied only when the patient is in a receptive frame of mind. A whole paper could be devoted to a discussion of how the patient's defenses must weaken so that he is willing and able to turn for help. To be direct when it is certain that such an approach will bounce off a shellproof exterior is obviously bad timing. It wastes ammunition that could later be effective. Other measures must be used first in an effort to soften these defenses. The direct approach can be ventured only when the patient is sufficiently vulnerable to make its success likely.

Secondly, what should be the doctor's attitude toward the patient's drinking during therapy? In the "platform" placed before the patient, I included a "wait-and-see plank." This I did for three reasons. In the first place, I did not want to give the impression of acting before I, too, was in possession of the facts about the drinking pattern. If it continued and caused difficulty, here was concrete evidence on which to base a decision about Antabuse.

A second reason for a tentative approach was the hope that the usual concept of the disciplinarian as dogmatic and arbitrary could be undercut if I adopted a less adamant program. If later on it became necessary to crack down, the patient would not be justified in claiming that the new tactics were evidence of a hopelessly closed mind toward drinking.

One patient tried to puncture that strategem by ferreting out the reason for the delaying tactics and accusing me of waiting until he had hung himself. Since that was true, I admitted the charge and went on from there. I told him he still had to look at the fact that he had hung himself. The focus was kept on the drinking problem that he still had to face.

The third reason for adopting a nondogmatic policy was to place myself in the position of being able to discuss the problem of the drinking with the patient directly. Generally with such delaying tactics the patient makes an extra effort at control and as a rule succeeds for a while, after which the condition usually takes its course and the patient gets drunk. At that point, it is possible to review with him his hopes of controlling intake and his consequent disillusionment and renewed awareness of his drinking problem. In this manner, the patient's feeling of need for help is revived and motivation is thereby strengthened. Therapy can thus proceed on a firmer footing.

My third comment opens up a vast area. It has to do with the significance of the direct approach in treating alcoholism or any other condition. The full import of this question can only be hinted, but an effort must be made to point out the far-reaching bearing of the direct approach with its stopping attribute.

One way to discuss the significance of being direct is to ask the question, "How much of the handling of people is of the direct or stopping variety?" To my mind the answer is, "Far more than most of us realize or have ever suspected." As already pointed out, incarceration is a form of direct treatment. It still has its values in certain situations. Its more respectable counterpart, the trip or vacation or residence in a sanatorium, serves much the same purpose, namely that of lifting the individual out of the whirling currents of his everyday existence and depositing him in a setting where he can slow down and stop.

One can also wonder at the new therapies. Certainly shock gives the body and mind an awful beating, which in some obscure fashion perhaps may serve a disciplinary, hence stopping, function. Again the sleep therapies put the patient in an enforced rest and, for the time being, effectively stop him.

Children are told to "cut that out" and know that they are being stopped. While the routine use of such a phrase is severely to be frowned upon, the teacher or person in authority who cannot use that phrase when necessary is badly handicapped in the performance of his job.

Youngsters in the nursery school or kindergarten reveal the need for stopping. Good practice has periods of free play interspersed with times when the children sit and draw or paint or listen to stories or have rest periods. These quiet times are designed to slow the youngsters down. On occasion, particularly with a new and inexperienced teacher, the class gets too keyed up and, since this kind of excitement is infectious, the class goes "wild." It then must be dismissed for the day. The firm hand of the good teacher was lacking, and the children got out of control.

Certainly a lot of preventive mental hygiene is of this same stopping variety. We sleep, we play, or take holidays to provide a break or a cut in the monotony of continued plugging. We seek avocational interests to change our life pattern. Part of the undoubted value of church attendance arises from the peace and quiet of the religious ceremonies and the soothing atmosphere of the church surroundings.

The list is long and could be expanded almost indefi-

nitely. Most rule-of-thumb therapy is of this sort. To rule
directness out because it is not scientific may hamstring
our effectiveness as people. Neither was surgery, which is
a "cut-it-out" technique, too scientific at the outset, but
its value was never doubted, and as it went on, the skill
in its application advanced until its use is now routine,
always, of course, where it is indicated. Yet, obviously,
surgery only tackles a symptom, a resultant of infection
or tissue change. The surgeon's concern with cause does
not hinder his taking appropriate action.

Similarly the psychiatrist should not hesitate to cut in.
He should not be just a butcher with a knife, but perhaps
more than is the custom, the psychiatrist should assume
responsibility for things happening to his patient. He
must not fall back on the excuse that his patient was un-
cooperative or poorly motivated; he must do his bit to
shift attitudes so that cooperation is obtained. Sometimes
a little discipline, artfully applied, works wonders. To discard it entirely may deprive one of a very necessary therapeutic resource.

Summary

In conclusion, let me repeat what I initially stated, namely
that the treatment of the alcoholic must include direct
treatment of the symptom. This does not exclude the
value of deep insights; it merely rechannels them into an
understanding of why the patient blocks from taking the
remedy prescribed. The study of causation is shifted from
origins to the causes that obstruct the therapy. As they are
uncovered and resolved, not only is sobriety attained but
the inner changes necessary to a sober existence can be
and are developed.

The truth of this last statement I can only vouch for at
this time. In a later paper I shall try to prove the validity

of this claim. In the meantime, this paper will have served its purpose if it has alerted the reader to the dangers inherent in the rigid application of the concept of symptomatic behavior and has tempered his antagonisms to disciplinary measures when properly applied. If it has, the effort to prepare it has been worthwhile.

Anonymity: The Ego Reducer[1]

Under ordinary circumstances I should thank the man who introduced me for his very nice remarks, but also for years I have been making a name for ego reduction. I'm not sure my ego got sufficiently reduced by the introduction.

When the invitation came to speak before this group, I immediately said yes, I want to go. For many years, as you all know, I have been associated with AA. All the experiences that I had had came flashing through my mind, and I had so much to say that I didn't quite know where to begin. And with your permission I am going to use a manuscript so that the points that I want to make will not be forgotten.

At an AA meeting, the speaker, as a rule, identifies himself as an alcoholic and then proceeds to tell his story, sprinkling garlands of wisdom, humor, or both as he goes along. I shall also tell my story, although I am much less sure about my matching either the wit or the wisdom of the AA speakers.

I joined AA by proxy in 1939, when a patient of mine became a member of the New York group. Well do I remember my first AA meeting. It was tinged with excitement. AA was going on the air for the first time. One of the members, trying to rehabilitate himself, had talked with Gabriel Heater, who, on hearing his story, suggested that he, the AA man, appear on the program *We the People*. This was a night far too thrilling and special for settling down to a regular meeting.

The actual event was a bit of a letdown. The man from AA spoke briefly of his experiences. Gabriel Heater, plainly puzzled, had a couple of pointless questions, and it was over. AA, however, had taken a step toward making itself known. Not a very big step to be sure, but one of the many that finally led to its present position on the national and international scene.

Later I attended other meetings more orthodox in character. As I did, I developed a conviction that the group had hit upon a method that solved the problem of excessive drinking. In a sense it was an answer to my prayers. After years of butting my head against the problem of treating the alcoholic, one could begin to hope.

In retrospect my first two or three years of contact with AA were the most exciting in my whole professional life. AA was then in its "miracle phase." Everything that happened seemed strange, wonderful. Hopeless drunks were being lifted out of the gutter. Individuals who had sought every known means of help without success were responding to this new approach. To be close to any such group, even by proxy, was electrifying.

In addition, professionally, a whole new avenue of problems of alcohol had opened up. Somewhere in the AA experience was the key to sobriety. There was the first authentic clue after many years of fruitless efforts. Needless to say, the possibilities ahead were most intriguing. Perhaps I could learn how AA worked and thus could learn something about how people stop drinking. All of which meant that I shared in the general excitement of those days. I could see some daylight ahead. My future in this regard was now clear: I would try to discover what made AA tick.

In this quest for understanding, I would have never gotten beyond first base, if it had not been for Bill and many of the early members. The study of the Twelve Steps helped a little. But of far greater importance were the many insights already possessed by Bill and the others into the process through which AA brought about its results. I heard of the need to hit bottom, of the necessity for accepting a Higher Power, of the indispensability of humility—ideas that had never crossed my professional horizon and certainly had never influenced my non-professional thinking or attitudes. Revolutionary as they were, these ideas, nevertheless, made sense, and I found myself embarked on a tour of discovery. I began to recognize more clearly what hitting bottom really implied. I began to do what I could to induce the experience in others, always wondering what was happening inside the individual as he went through the crisis of hitting bottom.

Finally fortune smiled upon me again, this time in the form of another patient. For some period she had been under my new brand of psychotherapy, designed to promote hitting bottom. For reasons completely unknown, she experienced a mild but typical conversion, which brought her into a positive state of mind. Led by her newly found spiritual elements, weak though they were, she started attending various churches in town. One Monday morning she entered my office, her eyes ablaze, and at once commenced talking. "I know what happened to me. I heard it in church yesterday. I surrendered."

With that word *surrender* she handed me my first real awareness of what happens during the period of hitting bottom. The individual is fighting the admission of being licked, of admitting that he is powerless. If and when he surrendered, he quit fighting, could admit he was licked, and could accept that he was powerless and needed help. If he did not surrender, a thousand crises could hit him, and nothing would happen. The need to induce surrender became the new therapeutic goal.

The miracle of AA was now a little clearer. For reasons still obscure, the program and the fellowship of AA could induce a surrender, which could in turn lead to a period of no drinking.

As might be expected, I too had a thrill of my own. I was getting in on what was happening, always an enjoyable experience. Still questing eagerly I shifted my therapeutic attack. The job now was to induce surrender. When I tried to cause that, I ran into a whole nest of resistances to that idea, totally new territory to be explored. As I continued my tour, it became ever more apparent that in everyone's psyche there existed an unconquerable ego that bitterly opposed any thought of defeat. Until that ego was somehow reduced or rendered ineffective, no likelihood of surrender could be anticipated.

The shift in emphasis from hitting bottom, to surrender, to ego reduction all occurred during the first five or six years after my initial contact with AA. I well remember the first AA meeting to which I spoke on the subject of ego reduction.

AA, still very much in its infancy, was celebrating the third or fourth anniversary of one of the groups. The speaker immediately preceding me told in detail of the efforts of his local group—which consisted of two men— to get him to dry up and become its third member. After several months of vain effort on their part and repeated nosedives on his, the speaker went on to say, "Finally I got cut down to size and have been sober ever since." His sobriety was a matter of some two or three years then.

When my turn came to speak, I used his phrase *cut down to size* as a text around which to weave my remarks. Before long, out of the corner of my eye, I was conscious of a disconcerting stare. It was coming from the previous speaker. Looking a little more directly, I could see his eyes fixed on me in open-eyed wonder. It was perfectly clear that he was utterly amazed that he had said anything that made sense to a psychiatrist. The look of incredulity never left his face for my entire talk.

The incident had one value in my eyes. It showed that two people, one approaching the matter clinically, and the other relying on his own intuitive report of what had happened to him, both came up with exactly the same observation: the need for ego reduction.

During the past decade, my own endeavors have centered primarily upon this problem of ego reduction. How far I have been able to explore that territory is not at all certain. I have, however, made a little progress. I shall try first to acquaint you with some of my findings, and second to relate them to the AA scene as I see it.

As I have already stated, the fact that hitting bottom could produce a surrender that cut the ego to size was evident fairly soon. In time, two additional facts manifested themselves. The first was that a reduced ego has marvelous recuperative powers. The second was that surrender is an essentially disciplinary function and experience. The first is merely repeating a fact known to you all. It is common knowledge that a return of the full-fledged ego can happen at any time. Years of sobriety are no insurance against its resurgence. No AA, regardless of his veteran status, can ever relax his guard against the encroachment of a reviving ego.

Recently one AA, writing to another, reported he was suffering, he feared from "halo-tosis," an obvious reference to the smugness and self-complacency that so easily can creep into the individual with years of sobriety behind him. The assumption that one has all the answers—

or the contrary, that one needs to know no answers and just follow AA—are two indicators of trouble. In both, open-mindedness is notably absent.

Perhaps as the commonest manifestation of the return of ego is witnessed in the individual who falls from his pink cloud, a state of mind familiar to you all. This blissful pink-cloud state is a logical aftermath of surrender. The ego, which is full of striving, just quits, and the individual senses peace and quiet within. The result is an enormous feeling of release, and the person flies right up to his pink cloud and thinks he has found heaven on earth. Everyone knows he is doomed to fall. But it is perhaps not equally clear that it is the ego, slowly making its comeback, that forces the descent from the pink cloud into the arena of life, where with the help of AA, he can learn how to become a sober person and not an angel.

I could go on with many more examples familiar to you all of the danger of ever assuming that the ego is dead and buried. Its capacity for rebirth is utterly astounding and must never be forgotten.

My second finding that surrender is a disciplinary experience requires explanation. In recent articles I have shown that the ego basically must be forging continuously ahead. It operates on the unconscious assumption that it, the ego, can never be stopped. It takes for granted its right to go ahead, and in this respect has no expectation of being stopped and no capacity to adjust to that eventuality. Stopping says, in effect, "No, you cannot continue," which is the essence of disciplinary control. The individual who cannot take a stopping is fundamentally an undisciplined person.

The function of surrender in AA is now clear. It produces that stopping by causing individuals to say, "I quit. I give up my headstrong ways. I've learned my lesson."

Very often for the first time in that individual's adult life [he has encountered] surrender and truly feels, "Thy will, not mine, be done." When that is true we have become, in fact, obedient servants of God. The spiritual life, at that point, is a reality. We have become members of the human race.

I have now presented the two points I wish to make, namely, first, the ego is revivable, and second, surrender is a disciplinary experience.

I next wish to assess their significance for AA as I see it. Primarily the two points say quite simply, "AA can never just be a miracle." The simple act of surrender can produce sobriety by its stopping effect upon the ego. Unfortunately, that ego will return unless the individual learns to accept a disciplined way of life, which means the tendency for ego comeback is permanently checked.

This is not new to AA members. They have learned that a single surrender is not enough. Under the wise leadership of the founding fathers, the need for continued endeavor to maintain that miracle has been steadily stressed. The Twelve Steps urge repeated inventory, not just one. And the Twelfth Step itself is a routine reminder that one must work at preserving sobriety. Moreover, it is referred to as Twelfth Step work, which is exactly what it is. By that time, the miracle is for the other fellow.

The Twelve Traditions are also part of the nonmiracle aspect of AA. They represent, as Bill has said, the meanings of the lessons of experience. They serve as guides for the inexperienced; in reality they check the ways of the innocent and unwary. They bring the individual down to earth and present him with the facts of reality. In their own fashion the Traditions say, "Pay heed to the teachings of experience, or you will court disaster." It is with reason that we talk of the sober voice of experience.

My stress on the nonmiracle elements of AA has a purpose. When I first made my acquaintance with AA, I rode the pink cloud with most of its members. I too went through a period of disillusionment and, fortunately for me, I came out with a faith far stronger than anything a pink cloud can supply. Mind you, I am not selling miracles short, they do loosen the individual up. I now know, however, the truth of the biblical saying, "By their works you shall know them." Only through hard toil and labor can lasting results be obtained.

As a consequence of the need for work to supplement any miracle, my interest in the nonmiracle features has grown. I can accept more truly the necessity of organization, of structure, which curb as well as guide. I believe there must be meetings like this one to provide a sense of belonging to a big working organization, of which each individual is but a part. And I believe that any group or individual who fails to participate in the enterprises of the organization is rendering himself and his group a disservice by not submitting to the disciplinary values inherent in those activities. He may be keeping the ego free of entanglements, but he is also keeping himself unstopped. His chances of remaining sober are not of a high order. He is really going it alone and is headed for another miracle—that may not come off the next time.

In closing let me reaffirm my proxy membership in AA. I have been in on its glowing start, and I've shared in its growing pains. And now I have reached the state of deep conviction in the soundness of the AA process, including its miracle aspect. I have tried to convey to you some of my observations on the nature of that process. I hope they will help in making the AA experience not just a miracle, but a way of life that is filled with eternal values. AA has, I can assure you, done just that for me.

When the Big "I" Becomes Nobody[1]

The AA program of help is touched with elements of true inspiration, and in no place is that inspiration more evident than in the selection of its name, Alcoholics Anonymous. Anonymity is of course of great protective value, especially to the newcomer, but my present target is to focus on the even greater value anonymity has in contributing to the state of humility necessary for the maintenance of sobriety in the recovered alcoholic.

My thesis is that anonymity, thoughtfully preserved, supplies two essential ingredients to that maintenance. The two ingredients, actually two sides of the same coin, are first, the preservation of a reduced ego and second, the continued presence of humility or humbleness. As stated in the Twelfth Tradition of AA, "Anonymity is the spiritual foundation of all our traditions," reminding each member to place "principles before personalities."

Many of you will wonder what that word *ego* means. It has so many definitions that the first task is to clarify the nature of the ego needing reduction.

This ego is not an intellectual concept but a state of feeling—a feeling of importance—of being "special." Few people can recognize this need to be special in themselves. Most of us, however, can recognize offshoots of this attitude and put the proper name to it. Let me illustrate. Early in the AA days, I was consulted about a serious problem plaguing the local group. The practice of celebrating a year's sobriety with a birthday cake had resulted in a certain number of members getting drunk within a short period after the celebration. It seemed apparent that some could not stand prosperity. I was asked to settle between birthday cakes and no birthday cakes. Characteristically, I begged off, not from shyness but from ignorance. Some three or four years later, AA furnished me the answer. The group no longer had such a problem because, as one member said, "We celebrate still, but a year's sobriety is now a dime a dozen. No one gets much of a kick out of that anymore!"

A look at what happened shows us ego, as I see it, in action. Initially, the person who had been sober for a full year was a standout, someone to be looked up to. His ego naturally expanded, his pride flowered; any previous deflation vanished. With such a renewal of confidence, he took a drink. He had been made special and reacted accordingly. Later, the special element dropped out. No ego feeds off being in the dime-a-dozen category, and the problem of ego buildup vanished.

Today, AA in practice is well aware of the dangers of singling anyone out for honors and praise. The dangers of reinflation are recognized. The phrase "trusted servant" is a conscious effort to keep that ego down, although admittedly some servants have a problem in that regard.

Now let us take a closer look at this ego, which causes trouble. The feelings associated with this state of mind are of basic importance in understanding the value of anonymity for the individual—the value of placing him in the rank and file of humanity.

Certain qualities typify this ego, which views itself as special and therefore different. It is "high" on itself and prone to keep its goals and visions at the same high level. It disdains what it sees as grubs who plod along lacking the fire and inspiration of those who are sparked by ideals that lift people out of the commonplace and offer promise of better things to come.

Often the same ego operates in reverse. It despairs of man with his faults and his failings, and develops a cynicism that sours the spirit and makes of its possessor a cranky realist who finds nothing good in this vale of tears. Life never quite meets his demands upon it, and he lives an embittered existence, grabbing what he can out of the moment but never really part of what goes on around him. He seeks love and understanding and prates endlessly about his sense of alienation from those around him. Basically, he is a disappointed idealist—forever aiming high and landing low. Both of these egos confuse humbleness with humiliation.

To develop this further, the expression "You think you're something" nicely catches the sense of being above the crowd. Children readily spot youngsters who think they are something and do their bests to puncture that illusion. For instance, they play a game called tag. In it, the one who is tagged is called "it." You've heard them accuse each other saying, "You think you're it," thereby charging the other with acting as though he was better than his mates. In their own way, children make very good therapists or head shrinkers. They are skillful puncturers of inflated egos, even though their purpose is not necessarily therapeutic.

AA had its start in just such a puncturing. Bill W. always refers to his experience at Towns Hospital as a "deflation in great depth" and on occasion has been heard to say that his ego took a "hell of a licking." AA stems from that deflation and that licking.

Clearly the sense of being special, of being "something," has its dangers, its drawbacks for the alcoholic. Yet the opposite, namely, that one is to be a nothing, has little counterappeal. The individual seems faced with being a something and getting drunk or being a nothing and getting drunk from boredom.

The apparent dilemma rests upon a false impression about the nature of nothingness as a state of mind. The ability to accept ourselves as nothing is not easily developed. It runs counter to all our desires for identity; for an apparently meaningful existence, one filled with hope and promise. To be nothing seems a form of psychological suicide. We cling to our somethingness with all the strength at our command. The thought of being a nothing is simply not acceptable. But the fact is that the person who does not learn to be as nothing cannot feel that he is but a plain, ordinary, everyday kind of person who merges with the human race—and as such is humble, lost in the crowd and essentially anonymous. When that can happen, the individual has a lot going for him.

People with "nothing" on their mind can relax, go about their business quietly and with a minimum of fuss and bother. They can even enjoy life as it comes along. In AA, this is called the twenty-four-hour program, which really signifies the fact that the individual does not have tomorrow on his mind. He can live in the present and find his pleasure in the here and now. He is hustling nowhere. With nothing on his mind, the individual is receptive and open-minded.

The great religions are conscious of the need for nothingness if one is to attain Grace. In the New Testament, Matthew, 18:3–4, quotes Christ with these words: "Truly, I say to you, unless you turn and become like children, you will never enter the kingdom of heaven. Whoever humbles himself like this child, he is the greatest in the kingdom of heaven."

Zen teaches the release of nothingness. A famous series of pictures designed to show growth in man's nature ends with a circle enclosed in a square. The circle depicts man in a state of nothingness . . . the square represents the framework of limitations man must learn to live within. In this blank state "Nothing is easy, nothing hard" and so Zen, too, has linked nothingness, humbleness, and Grace.

Anonymity is a state of mind of great value to the individual in maintaining sobriety. While I recognize its protective function, I feel that any discussion of it would be one-sided if it failed to emphasize the fact that the maintenance of a feeling of anonymity—of a feeling of "I am nothing special"—is a basic insurance of humility and so a basic safeguard against further trouble with alcohol. This kind of anonymity is truly a precious possession.

Treating the *Causes* of Alcoholism[1]

I liked the article "An AA Doctor's Prescription," which appeared in [a previous] issue of the *Grapevine*. It nicely stressed the importance of stopping the symptom of drinking. The picture showing the roots and fruits of alcoholism is graphic and intelligible. The concept "The treatment of a symptom is," I am sure, a sound one.

The emphasis on the removal of the symptom can, however, be misleading. It suggests a failure to reach the fundamentals and implies that the symptomatic cure leaves the individual skating on thin ice with the underlying causes of the trouble still lurking in the background ready at any moment to trip up the individual. The charge of superficiality may well be levied against a treatment that thinks only in terms of symptoms.

The truth, however, is that routinely to assume superficiality is also an error. Sometimes, the treatment of a symptom hits into the deeper structures while it takes care of the symptom itself.

The history of medicine is dotted with examples in which the remedy of a symptom provided the cure of the condition. A classic illustration is malaria. The malarial patient had a symptom, a fever. Quinine cured this fever and was in use over the centuries, long before the cause had been determined. The therapy was completely symptomatic yet, as is now known, actually has a scientific basis: the malarial parasite was killed by the drug.

In other words, treatment, discovered by chance in nature, in a funny sense, reversed the usual sequence.

Science says first find the cause and remedy that, thus curing the illness. Instead, the use of quinine treated the symptom of fever with no reference to the cause, which only later was revealed. The charge of superficiality was disproved by facts uncovered subsequently.

AA is also a therapy discovered by chance. To be sure, the original members followed brilliantly the clues with which their own experience had presented them. They learned from experiencing; they followed no book. They found a method, a program; they prescribed it and it worked. The idea of seeking causes was discarded, sometimes noisily and with jeers at those who still tried to be scientific.

Yet AA, like quinine, was designed not only to cure the symptom of drinking but also to tackle and, if possible, eradicate its causes. The AA program helped the individual remain sober, thus removing the symptoms. It also aimed at altering the inner source of discord by its stress on spiritual development, thereby getting at the causes that provoked the symptoms.

The fact is that, as spiritual growth proceeds, the underlying hostile elements are steadily reduced in strength, and thus, in their capacity to cause trouble. Psychiatric therapy, depending upon analytic concepts, had tried to reach and uproot the hidden hostilities that poisoned the psyche, the assumption being that such unearthing would free the individual from their grip and enable him to pursue a more healthy path. Unfortunately, the uncovering method had no way of ensuring removal. The individual became acquainted with his hostilities and had no means of getting rid of them.

AA adopted a very different approach. AA found a very basic fact, namely, that spiritual growth is the real antidote for the hostile, negative forces. It learned that these feelings do not have to be uncovered but that somehow the spiritual elements can neutralize the negative forces, thus freeing the individual from their grip. In that way, the cause of the condition is effectively extirpated. Like quinine, which actually killed the organism, AA through its spiritual emphasis actually may succeed in ridding the individual of harmful attitudes and feelings that had contributed to his difficulties. AA, so to speak, cures without uncovering.

The point of my comment has now been made. AA is not to be considered merely a symptomatic remedy. Through its stress on the spiritual, it really digs much deeper. Like quinine, it tackles the original causes. Unfortunately, here the parallel ends. The malarial parasite is specific and can be destroyed. The evils with which the spiritual element must contend are not so readily wiped out. The most one can hope for is progress in the amelioration of the hostilities and growth in the positive forces that ensure health.

As a result of this thinking about AA and how its program works, I would like to suggest a companion picture. The tree would have a trunk with roots and branches. The trunk would be labeled the spiritual life and/or sobriety. The roots would have titles like love, warmth, charity, gratitude, friendship, forgiveness, kindliness. The limbs would be covered with leaves or blossoms and would indicate somehow the overflowing horn of plenty, the abundant life. This, as I see it, is the miracle not only of AA but of all life—the capacity to move from a negative to a positive way of life.

One final point, this time about how the psychiatrist fits into this picture. In my eyes, his is a dual task. He can help to remove blocks, i.e., the hostilities to spiritual growth, and also do what he can to foster the processes that lead to that growth. Unless he is mindful of both aspects, he is likely to be of little help. He can no more afford to overlook the spiritual than can any member of AA.

Why Psychiatrists Fail
with Alcoholics[1]

While no one is more convinced than I am that alcoholism is a disease, no one is more appalled than I am at the blithe manner with which the concept has been received and the easy use to which it has been put. To paraphrase Winston Churchill's famous war statement, I could say, "Never has so much been done on so little with so much hullabaloo."

I can say this quite frankly. I was in on the early hullabaloo and did a certain amount of it myself. I cannot help but feel that the whole field of alcoholism is way out on a limb that any minute will crack and drop us all in a frightful mess. I sometimes tremble to think of how little we have to back up our claims.

Yet actually I would not have it otherwise, nor do I think it could have happened differently. All movements get under way through some one or some group taking a chance. That has to be. The only danger comes from failure, later on, to see things in perspective. We should never be fooled by our own ballyhoo into any false sense about our accomplishments. The need to do something about alcoholism is admitted; the main question concerns the tools we have available to carve out satisfactory results. To me they still seem pretty crude and makeshift.

This fact, while it is to be deplored, cannot be used to condemn. It is an outgrowth of forces over which we as a group had little or no control. The field, like Topsy, just "growed." First it was the Research Council, then it was the people at Yale and the mighty impetus of Alcoholics Anonymous. Finally it was the organizational and educational work of the National Committee on Alcoholism. The question now is what do we face—those of us who are actively engaged in meeting the problem?

Have we not almost promised to do a job with very little real right to say anything more than "we'll try"? Have enough of our energies been devoted to helping us get down off that limb—toward establishing a reliable body of data and experience that will enable us to develop competent practitioners in the field of alcoholism? I very much doubt it.

There are undoubtedly many reasons for this failure to establish reliable information about alcoholism. One, however, strikes me as of great importance because it is subtle and not generally recognized: the fact that persons who enter the field of alcoholism come from other fields. More than they realize, they are bringing something to the field and have little expectation of learning anything from the field, nor do they feel any particular need to do this. They have already been taught; now they will apply what they know. It does not take them long to realize that what they know does not amount to much when it comes to handling alcoholics.

Two reactions are then possible. The individual either changes and begins to function, or he remains rigid and becomes discouraged, disillusioned, and skeptical about the prospects of working with the alcoholic. The unfortunate truth is that, as far as psychiatrists are concerned, a sizable majority never quite make the grade. They always seem like fish out of water.

Naturally I have given thought to this new phenomenon. My explanation lies in the point of view they bring with them. They come equipped with training, and they busily engage themselves in trying to utilize their equipment. Rarely does it function well in the field of alcoholism. The question is: "Why, when that same equipment serves well in other areas, does it fail them with alcoholics?"

I think this is an important question. One reason for the lack of specific knowledge about alcoholism is the dearth of clinicians who remain in the field long enough to obtain any feel for the condition. They seldom get beyond the dabbling stage and are in no position to add to our knowledge. In the summary of the research meeting held in October 1954, Diethelm[2] stated that most investigators in alcoholism reported once and then quit, confirming my own observations. We must ask the question, "What happens to produce this repeated development?"

This question and its predecessor, "Why does the well-equipped psychiatrist fail with alcoholics?" can, I believe, be answered by the same reply. Before trying to formulate an answer, let me set the stage with some background material. The present-day psychiatrist is steeped in the methods of modern medicine. Whenever you encounter illness, you search for the cause and cure the illness. That is just as true for psychiatric ailments as it is for physical conditions. Treatment is directed toward etiology.

When a person so oriented hits alcoholism, he is out of luck—only he does not know it. What happens is that he bypasses the disease and looks for causes; he ends up talking about earlier experiences and never gets close to this patient or the illness. His training is a hindrance instead of a help. He must revamp his sights, or he is lost.

At a meeting last winter, a psychiatrist thoroughly trained in the modern approach read a paper in which he outlined some of the thinking that he had to scrap before he could operate comfortably with alcoholic patients. He stressed mostly the need to give up history taking and deep search for causes, particularly at the start of any therapeutic relationship. During the discussion that followed, he was chided by a more orthodox colleague who was a bit horror-struck at the heresy about history taking. The reply of the reader of the paper was in my eyes perfect. He said in part, "I used to think a full history was necessary but I found it didn't work; I had to change my mind." Needless to say this person is continuing in the field of alcoholism and I believe will be heard from again. He did not adhere rigidly to his training precepts; he really accepted reality and to that extent was more effective. Unfortunately, there are not many of his kind.

What happened, of course, was that he shifted his sights and looked at the illness alcoholism, which he was finding could not be treated by the conventional approach he had learned. He had to formulate a new approach. How he did that I cannot tell you. I can tell you, however, about how I have modified my own thinking in the light of experiences similar to those of the man I have been talking about.

Perhaps the first thing to impress me with the need to change my approach was the routine complaint from patients that their talks with psychiatrists were almost uniformly unhelpful. This was in the earlier days. The complaint was that the psychiatrists never talked about the drinking and seemed to minimize its importance, which was duck soup for the alcoholic, but, in the long run, not very effective. The routine history-taking approach seemed to have many strikes against it.

Then secondly, AA came along with a program to stop drinking; causation was ignored, the focus was all on treatment. Medicine's insistence on treating causes was disregarded, not wittingly to be sure, but the emphasis was on stopping the drinking and helping the individual to achieve and maintain that end. Like the treatment by surgery, the causes were irrelevant in meeting the immediate issues. Instead of the scalpel, there was the AA program. Instead of the infected appendix being removed, the individual was told to stop drinking, or stated in another way, liquor was removed from his life.

In the old days, patients were given remedies such as digitalis to help correct or overcome the symptom, namely, the weakened heart muscle. Remedial treatment nowadays tends to be downgraded as temporizing and superficial. It lacks precision and seems a blunderbuss method. Yet no one is willing to discard digitalis, and no one that I know of is going to urge the scrapping of AA. They both work, they both preserve life, and though neither cures, both provide for the prolongation of life and thus add years of satisfying existence. For people so benefited, interest in causation is academic. The clinician may wish he knew more about causes, but he is grateful for the fact that he has a remedy. And almost always he wishes he had more of them.

Similarly, any treatment of the alcoholic must be remedial. There is no present value in getting at the causes and correcting them because the net result of such an endeavor would be to enable the person to drink normally. While such a goal may be achieved in some far-off millennium, its attainment in the immediate future is absolutely unlikely. Any therapy devoted to such a goal is admittedly unrealistic; everyone acknowledges that there is no present cure, that the only remedy is total sobriety. The person does not learn how to handle liquor, he stops using it.

The goal of therapy is, therefore, to get the patient to stop taking the first drink. I have found it fruitful to work along the line of why the patient will not or cannot stop taking that first drink. It has led to the concepts of hitting bottom (adopted, of course, from AA), surrender, compliance, and recognition of an intractable ego that will not stop for anyone or anything. And strangely enough, in trying to apply the remedy of stopping drinking, I have learned more about the alcoholic and his problem than I ever did when I was concentrating on causes and minimizing all remedial efforts.

Once I concentrated on trying to stop the drinking, I began to focus on the illness itself, which took on more and more stature as a disease. Finally, I was willing to set aside my previous experience and center attention upon what was going on that was ill or sick. The clinical situation held my nose to the grindstone, and it was from the clinical situation I learned about alcoholism. And I know that as soon as I divorce myself from the clinical situation my source of learning will be gone.

Now is not the time to talk about the remedies we have available. You know them as well as I do. The real problem is to get the individual to take those remedies. Unless one is practiced in handling the various dodges or stratagems of the alcoholic, one gets nowhere. Defense reactions are found in every psychological illness. The alcoholic has the same defenses as others plus a sturdy crop of his own, arising from the special nature of his ailment. Until the practitioner develops some dexterity in penetrating the wall surrounding the alcoholic, he can anticipate little progress.

Articles on how to establish contact with the alcoholic in order to get him to accept possible remedies are scarcer than hen's teeth. Should there be pressure or not is an everyday issue. Do we have any consensus of opinion? What has experience taught? Too often the voice of the clinician is muted because all he can offer is his own experience, which seems pretty feeble compared with the authoritative voice of statistics. Yet all the statistics in the world will never provide one with clinical judgment nor aid one in the practice of one's trade or profession.

In the field of alcoholism, we need more people who will report their experiences as practitioners so that gradually a body of accepted practice can slowly be acquired. The knowledge of that practice and the ability to apply it will enable the individual to be expert in the field. Not until he has that knowledge can he be called expert, no matter how thoroughly trained he may be in the same allied field.

We can now answer the question raised previously, namely, "Why do psychiatrists fail so frequently with alcoholics?" The answer is that they fail to adopt a remedial approach and consequently are pretty much strangled as therapists. Not until they know that they are tackling a disease that must be treated for itself can they hope to be effective.

My plea, of course, is for more serious study of the illness alcoholism. My interest is not so much in causation as in the recognition of a disease that must be treated by remedial measures. My hope is that as the focus is kept on the disease, the practice of handling the disease will receive even greater study and consideration. I believe that only in that way will the field be able to climb off the limb it now occupies and reach solid ground, where it can meet its obligations with some degree of consistency.

We must stop borrowing from other disciplines and develop our own body of knowledge and experience.

Notes

Introduction

1. "Dr. Tiebout, a Leader in Study of Alcoholics," *New York Herald Tribune,* Monday, 4 April 1966.

In Memory of Harry

1. Reprinted, with permission, from the *AA Grapevine* 1, no. 2 (July 1966): 2–4. Copyright © by the AA Grapevine, Inc.

2. H. M. Tiebout, "The Ego Factors in Surrender in Alcoholism," *Quarterly Journal of Studies on Alcohol* 15, no. 4 (December 1954): 610–21.

The Role of Psychiatry in the Field of Alcoholism, with Comment on the Concept of Alcoholism as Symptom and as Disease

1. Revised from an address presented to the American Psychiatric Association, Montreal, May 7, 1949. Reprinted, with permission, from *Quarterly Journal of Studies on Alcohol* 12, no. 1 (March 1951, presently *Journal of Studies on Alcohol*): 52–57. Copyright Journal of Studies on Alcohol, Inc., Rutgers Center of Alcohol Studies, Piscataway, NJ 08854.

2. For the basic idea of this analogy I am indebted to Professor E. M. Jellinek, who has elaborated it in his lectures to students at the Yale Summer School of Alcohol Studies.

The Act of Surrender in the Therapeutic Process, with Special Reference to Alcoholism

1. Reprinted, with permission, from *Quarterly Journal of Studies on Alcohol* 10, no. 1 (June 1949, presently *Journal of Studies on Alcohol*):

48–58. Copyright Journal of Studies on Alcohol, Inc., Rutgers Center of Alcohol Studies, Piscataway, NJ 08854.

Surrender versus Compliance in Therapy, with Special Reference to Alcoholism

1. Reprinted, with permission, from *Quarterly Journal of Studies on Alcohol* 14, no. 1 (March 1953, presently *Journal of Studies on Alcohol*): 58–68. Copyright Journal of Studies on Alcohol, Inc., Rutgers Center of Alcohol Studies, Piscataway, NJ 08854.

2. L. R. Sillman, "Chronic Alcoholism," *Journal of Nervous and Mental Disorders* 107 (1948): 127–49.

3. H. M. Tiebout, "Therapeutic Mechanisms of Alcoholics Anonymous," *American Journal of Psychiatry* 100 (1944): 468–73.

4. H. M. Tiebout, "The Act of Surrender in the Therapeutic Process, with Special Reference to Alcoholism," *Quarterly Journal of Studies on Alcohol* 10, no. 1 (June 1949): 48–58.

5. M. Grayson, "Concept of 'Acceptance' in Physical Rehabilitation," *Journal of the American Medical Association* 145 (1951): 893–96.

6. "Alcoholism Treatment Digest: Alcoholics Anonymous," *Connecticut Review on Alcoholism* 3 (1952): 39–40.

7. L. S. Kubie, *Practical and Theoretical Aspects of Psychoanalysis* (New York: International Unversities Press, 1950).

The Ego Factors in Surrender in Alcoholism

1. Reprinted, with permission, from *Quarterly Journal of Studies on Alcohol* 15, no. 4 (December 1954, presently *Journal of Studies on Alcohol*): 610–21. Copyright Journal of Studies on Alcohol, Inc., Rutgers Center of Alcohol Studies, Piscataway, NJ 08854.

2. H. M. Tiebout, "The Act of Surrender in the Therapeutic Process, with Special Reference to Alcoholism," *Quarterly Journal of Studies on Alcohol* 10, no. 1 (June 1949): 48–58.

3. H. M. Tiebout, "Surrender versus Compliance in Therapy, with Special Reference to Alcoholism," *Quarterly Journal of Studies on Alcohol* 14, no. 1 (March 1953): 58–68.

4. S. Radó , "The Psychoanalysis of Pharmachothymia (Drug

Addiction): The Clinical Picture," *Psychoanalysis Quarterly* 2 (1933): 1–23.

    5. Radó , "The Psychoanalysis of Pharmachothymia."

Alcoholics Anonymous: An Experiment of Nature

    1. Revised from an address presented at the New York Medical Society on Alcoholism, October 6, 1959. Reprinted, with permission, from *Quarterly Review of Studies on Alcohol* 22, no. 1 (March 1961, presently *Journal of Studies on Alcohol*): 52–68. Copyright Journal of Studies on Alcohol, Inc., Rutgers Center of Alcohol Studies, Piscataway, NJ 08854.

    2. H. M. Tiebout, "Therapeutic Mechanisms of Alcoholics Anonymous," *American Journal of Psychiatry* 100 (1944): 468–73.

    3. S. Freud, *Collected Papers,* vol. IV (London: Hogarth Press, 1925).

    4. S. Radó, "The Psychoanalysis of Pharmachothymia (Drug Addiction): The Clinical Picture," *Psychoanalysis Quarterly* 2 (1933): 1–23.

    5. Freud, *Collected Papers.*

    6. Radó, "The Psychoanalysis of Pharmachothymia."

Direct Treatment of a Symptom

    1. Condensed from *Problems of Addiction and Habituation* (New York: Grune and Stratton, 1973).

    2. H. M. Tiebout, "Therapeutic Mechanisms of Alcoholics Anonymous," *American Journal of Psychiatry* 100 (1944): 468–73.

Anonymity: The Ego Reducer

    1. Speech presented at the Second International AA Convention, St. Louis, July 1955. Audiocassette transcription.

When the Big "I" Becomes Nobody

    1. Reprinted, with permission, from the *AA Grapevine* 22, no. 4 (September 1965): 2–5. Copyright © by the AA Grapevine, Inc.

Treating the *Causes* of Alcoholism

1. Reprinted, with permission, from the *AA Grapevine* 20, no. 6 (November 1963): 9–11. Copyright © by the AA Grapevine, Inc.

Why Psychiatrists Fail with Alcoholics

1. From a speech presented at the National States Conference on Alcoholism, Miami. Reprinted from the *AA Grapevine* 13, no. 4 (September 1956): 5–10.

2. Oskar Diethelm, "Current Research on Problems of Alcoholism: Report of the Section of Psychiatric Research," *Quarterly Journal of Studies on Alcohol* 16, no. 3 (September 1955): 574.

Other titles that may interest you . . .

Ebby
The Man Who Sponsored Bill W.
by Mel B.
This book uncovers the life of Ebby Thacher, focusing on his role in the development of the Alcoholics Anonymous fellowship. It includes the message of recovery that Ebby Thacher gave to Bill W., cofounder of AA.
176 pages   Order no. 5699

Not-God
A History of Alcoholics Anonymous
by Ernest Kurtz
This book is a comprehensive, candid, truly definitive history of the creation, development, and legacy of Alcoholics Anonymous.
450 pages   Order no. 1036

New Wine
The Spiritual Roots of the Twelve Step Miracle
by Mel B.
This book combines the cultural currents of the nineteenth and twentieth centuries with the influences of numerous people and organizations to explore the miracle that is AA.
204 pages   Order no. 5080

For price and order information or a free catalog, please call our telephone representatives or visit our Web site at www.hazelden.org

◼ HAZELDEN®

1-800-328-9000
(Toll-Free U.S., Canada, and the Virgin Islands)

1-651-213-4000
(Outside the U.S. and Canada)

1-651-213-4590
(24-Hour Fax)

www.hazelden.org

15251 Pleasant Valley Road
P.O. Box 176
Center City, MN 55012-0176